Santis O'Garro is a lifecoach, entrepreneur and a social-media money mentor. Finding herself in debt up to her eyeballs and a newly single mother, she started the popular Instagram account The Caribbean Dub to share her journey of clearing €15,027 of debt, and she has since amassed 28.5k followers. She is a co-presenter of RTÉ's hit TV show *The Price of Everything* and a financial columnist for *Irish Country Magazine*.

THE MONEY MENTOR

THE MONEY MENTOR

How to Manage Debt,
Reach Your Goals
and Achieve Financial Wellness

SANTIS O'GARRO

HarperCollins*Ireland*

HarperCollins*Ireland*
Macken House
39/40 Mayor Street Upper
Dublin 1
D01 C9W8
Ireland

A division of
HarperCollins*Publishers*
1 London Bridge Street
London SE1 9GF
UK

www.harpercollins.co.uk

First published by HarperCollins*Publishers* 2023

1 3 5 7 9 10 8 6 4 2

A catalogue record for this book is available from the British Library

ISBN: 978-0-00-852319-0

Typeset in Futura by Palimpsest Book Production Ltd,
Falkirk, Stirlingshire

Printed and bound in the UK using 100% Renewable
Electricity by CPI Group (UK) Ltd

TThis book is produced from independently certified FSC™ paper
to ensure responsible forest management.

For more information visit: www.harpercollins.co.uk/green

I proudly dedicate this book to my children and those who feel that life is one financial firefighting mission. May you dare to dream and know that if you are reading this you already have a 100 per cent survival rate. Maybe it's time you dare to thrive.

CONTENTS

INTRODUCTION:

ORIGINS

I grew up on the Emerald Isle – not Ireland, but Montserrat, a small island in the Caribbean that is a British colony. It was called Montserrat after Christopher Columbus spotted it as he sailed to America on his second voyage. He named it after the Abbey of Montserrat in Spain. Montserrat has a unique connection to Ireland that many Irish people aren't aware of. I have listened to stories passed down from generation to generation about this connection between these two places. It is not a beautiful history in parts but it is ours and I think it's important that I share it.

From as early as I could remember, St Patrick's Day was always a day of celebration. We would wear green or our national Madras dresses and head into town and party in the carnival. It would be festivities all week long. As a child growing up in Montserrat, there was nothing I lived for more. This day was a big deal, and I didn't even really know why. Who was St Patrick? Patrick, that was a strange name. Apparently he got rid of the snakes in Ireland, but in Montserrat there were still lots of snakes so why were we thanking him? And believe me, I would've been the first to

1

thank him because I have such a massive fear of snakes. These are the questions I would constantly ask, but no one was forthcoming with answers.

Then my mom met Dermot, or Donut as we used to think he was called (because on a small Caribbean island, that name was pretty uncommon), and my whole family fell in love with him. To cut a long story short, we all moved to Dublin in May 1995. For some reason, even though we were in Ireland, St Patrick's Day was never the same. There was just a line of people walking through the streets, or people getting drunk everywhere. Where was the dancing, the street-food stalls, the celebration, the carnival and why was Montserrat one of the only other countries in the world where St Patrick's Day was a public bank holiday? What connected these two totally different worlds and cultures?

Many Irish people were actually sent as indentured servants, or willingly went to work in Montserrat during Cromwellian times, either forced or choosing to work on the British plantations there. By the middle of the seventeenth century, about 70 per cent of the population in Montserrat were actually Irish. As time went by, the Irish began to become planters instead of labourers, and the African slaves did the labour. As the years passed, the enslaved Africans came to outnumber their Irish masters, and on 17 March, 1768 – partly because they knew their masters would be celebrating St Patrick's Day – the slaves planned an uprising to gain their freedom.

Today on Montserrat we celebrate St Patrick's Day in honour of those who lost their lives in that uprising, and because we Montserratians consider ourselves the Black Irish of the Caribbean.

I had a happy upbringing in Montserrat, split between two households. It was a case of two Roses. One Rose was my mother, and the other was my godmother, Rose. Looking back, their perspectives on money were quite different and I guess – without being aware of it at the time – that this is where I got my earliest lesson about finances. Growing up in Montserrat for the first ten years of my life was an adventure. Looking back, we were poor, but we didn't live in poverty. It is hard to explain this. You couldn't starve in Montserrat because there was an abundance of fruit, nuts and seafood. The land was good for farming because of the fertility of the volcanic soil. (Incidentally, the volcano on Montserrat would erupt in 1995, two months after my arrival in Ireland, changing the island forever.) I loved books and would often create adventures with my brothers taken from my favourite book, *Huckleberry Finn*, written by Mark Twain. I loved my life there and even when things were lean, we survived.

While life in Montserrat was good, my financial education wasn't. The only thing I remember about money from my time there was that there wasn't much of it at home, and we just made do. My mam was honest and hardworking, and I was smart enough to know that people with loads of money didn't have to work two jobs like she did. For me as a child, having money meant living ostentatiously. The people I saw who had money – or who I *thought* had money – were the ones with gold chains and rings, or the new Jordans sent to them by family in America. Nowadays I like to look back on my life as if material things never mattered to me, but in retrospect, they did. Although we had family abroad, we weren't supported in that sense. My mother worked hard, and she had various jobs in a bakery, a pizza parlour, and as a tiler as well as side hustles to make ends meet.

My godmother Rose was good with money. Although she wasn't flashy, she was very savvy. She had land, a house and a shop. When I was in her house there were no worries about anything, except maybe going to church on time. The strange thing is, looking back, she had more financial security than the gold-chain flashers, but I never associated her with being financially well off.

Whether my family had money or not, I had a happy childhood in the Caribbean, and I can see now that it's where my resourcefulness came from. I would collect and pound almonds and swap them for the jellies and sweets sold in my favourite sweetshop, Sister Boston's. I might not have known how to budget back then, but I learned how to hustle.

But unfortunately, even though lack of money never bothered me, I was bullied at school for having very little. Even if this is hard to admit, I would've loved to have worn Reeboks or been one of the cool gangs. I think this level of self-awareness at a young age was a catalyst for me, the start of my feeling that I was never good enough and that only those with extra money could ever be part of the cool gang. One of my earliest memories is of turning up to netball practice in patent leather shoes with a foam sole. A boy on the side-lines asked why my mother wouldn't buy me proper shoes, and my whole team laughed.

It was humiliating.

Although playing netball was still more important to me back then than sly comments, I told myself that no one would ever laugh at me for not having things again.

This aspiration was short-lived, however, when I moved to Ireland.

In just three weeks I went from walking around Montserrat with pride to realising how uncool I was in every single way when I arrived in Dublin. Wrong colour, wrong attitude, wrong accent and wrong clothes.

You need to understand that I came from reading *Huckleberry Finn* and taking my two younger brothers on adventures to pick crayfish, mangoes, guavas and coconuts. Those were my favourite days. In Ireland, no one seemed to care about those things; no one seemed interested in those stories. I loved foraging, but what could you forage in a terrace house on the Northside of Dublin? I felt odd.

I was odd.

My peers in Ireland talked about the latest runners, or whose mam loved them the most because of what they bought. Everyone assumed I was poor, that I was like the people on the Trócaire boxes. Even at that age I knew the difference between not having a lot and being in poverty. That box, with its images of poverty porn, still haunts me. The grim reminders that we needed to give money to the little black babies in Africa left me with no choice but to prove to those around me that they weren't feeding me.

I had to show them that I was different. My inability to

communicate my feelings about this to anyone left me with an appetite to prove myself. And prove myself I did.

I worked my first job at age thirteen, on a milk round, where I saved and bought my first pair of Nike Air Max. I still remember when a girl who was older than me spotted them and commented, 'Wow, I love your runners.' That was it. I was finally accepted. Work hard, I learned, and you can buy whatever you want. Cue the beginnings of my money personality type – being a spender. There will be more on these personality types a little later.

I didn't learn about debt at home. If I'm honest, ours was the home where little by little we worked at things and got things done. I saw my mam and dad take handed-down couches until they could afford to buy their own. They weren't opposed to debt and would have seen credit union loans and credit unions as a positive route to go down. My dad actually never had a credit union loan or a credit card until later in life. I put that down to his upbringing: it just wasn't an option or a solution. You worked hard for what you had and I was raised to feel that it was wise to be prudent with money.

My first real financial influences in terms of taking on debt were my friends. I guess we were on the periphery of the Celtic Tiger boom and programmes such as Footballers' Wives and the glamourous Wags were aspirational to us young, working-class kids. My first encounter with debt was a holiday loan for £750, which led me on to a very dependent relationship between me and my credit union.

I got a buzz from two things: getting the loan and spending the money.

I eagerly filled out my first credit card application as a twenty-year-old. I was delighted to see my name on that shiny new card. It meant having extra money and offered an opportunity to go to the city centre every Thursday and put a dent in it. A new outfit and I was ready for the ultimate night out. I don't know why, but I felt euphoric when I got approved for a loan or credit and even more euphoric when I spent the money. I felt SEEN, LOVED and POWERFUL.

To this day, I still get that feeling; it doesn't come from actually having the products at the end of the purchase, but from everything leading up to that. I feel powerful; it makes my inner child feel worthy and accomplished. It's the steps of walking into a shop, the buzz in the air, even the salespeople packing my products up and the moment I am just about to pay; that's pure endorphin bliss.

As my twenties went by and I started to take on debt, I felt great wearing the clothes and driving a nice car, but I wasn't really buying any of these things for myself. I know this. I was trying to appease that inner child, because no matter what she acquired she always felt as if she was an outsider. Retail was therapy and debt funded my therapy.

At twenty-four I bought an apartment with my then-boyfriend. To be honest, I bought that apartment because my friends had begun travelling and I didn't want to follow them to Australia. My boyfriend also said he didn't want to travel. We looked around, and anyone in our circle that wasn't travelling was buying a house. So we saved and bought a house too. I took out the most significant loan of my life because I didn't want to travel. I am tied to a mortgage for thirty years because I didn't want to travel for a year. I stayed in my job for an extra thirteen years for the same reason.

Up to that point, buying a house was not something I dreamt of doing. Don't get me wrong, I was blessed to get a mortgage, but I was never grateful. I took it in my stride because it was just another badge of honour on my debt-acquiring career. If I had a grand plan for my dreams, buying a house at twenty-four would not have been it. If I really wanted a house, I would have researched the steps to get a mortgage and what types of mortgages were available to me. How much deposit did I want to have? Instead, I walked into a bank, did what was needed and never once had the knowledge or confidence to say, wait a minute, is this right for me? Is this part of my plan? Even as a 24 year-old woman with a great job, it was somewhat of an honour to get a loan. Believe me, I worked hard for it. I just didn't see it the way most people did. I believed that people like me didn't get opportunities to own their own homes, so I should take it. When that mortgage got approved, I had never experienced a buzz like it in my life – not until the birth of my children.

I bought my apartment for the wrong reasons. I worked hard, saved hard and convinced myself I was being financially mature, but of course I wasn't. It was the most significant loan of my life, but I had no concept of what getting a mortgage really meant. Luckily the apartment turned out okay, although it would go on to cause many headaches in the years to come.

My then-boyfriend and I bought the apartment in August 2007, on the eve of a recession that would last nearly a decade. How did I deal with that news? I got another loan. This time it was for home improvements, but instead of using it for what we needed, we flew to Barbados and St Lucia on holidays, because that was how I dealt with everything. I would carry on this pattern throughout my life. When our relationship eventually broke down, I bought an Audi A4 cabriolet to make sure my ex saw that I was doing okay.

I continued in a pattern of acquiring debt until life came to a head, as it invariably does. And when it rains, it pours. In October 2018, before I began my debt-free journey, it felt like things were starting to fall apart. I had two babies in the house, and it was getting into the cold of winter. As the weeks went by, my apartment began to smell and feel damp. I couldn't figure out why this was happening to my home. It took three weeks to locate the problem – the people in the apartment above had a leak in their kitchen, which flowed down through the walls and slowly ruined the wooden floors in my apartment. The leak did most of its damage to the storage room and the hallway, but I had the same flooring throughout the apartment, so ripping up the hallway would mean I would have to replace the floors throughout.

At this point I was already avoiding my bills and living with a constant lack of funds. When payday came around, I was deep in the red before my wages even hit my account. Needless to say, I was not too fond of payday. I called the maintenance man, and he suggested I get my dad, a carpenter, to fit the floors. I was even nervous to call the maintenance man because I was a good few thousand in arrears with my property management company. As I was totting up the figures in my head, I knew I would have to get decent underlay for the floor, which meant even more expense. And the floors would be €1500 minimum. Where was I going to get the money? To add to all this, my dad had only recently complained about his back, so I felt bad asking him to supply the labour for the job; chances were that I would have to find a fitter for the wooden floor, so that was another cost.

I had so many sleepless nights trying to figure out how to get the floor refitted. Money worries were a constant, uninvited guest into my head at that time. The credit union would not give me any more money as the loan I had was already high. All the while, my mind was constantly racing trying to figure out how I would repay the debt and also feed my children. This leak became one of three things that would ultimately lead to me having a psychological breakdown: apartment repairs were mounting up; my relationship was breaking down; and the death of my grandfather.

In January of 2018, I had split from my children's father and become a single mother. As the year went on my money worries just seemed to worsen. Finally, I joined an MLM (multi-level marketing – also known as a pyramid scheme), hoping it would better my situation, but I went further into debt. I remember in March of that year there was a snow-storm, and I made a big pot of soup for my son and me. It was nerve-wracking as I saw others stocking up, but that wasn't an option in our house. Nobody wants to avoid the post box for fear of another bill, or stay up late riddled with anxiety, but that's where I was at that moment.

In a country like Ireland, I never thought that I – a working woman who could buy her own home – would be reduced to choosing between topping up my electricity and buying formula for my youngest child. On the outside my life looked fine, as I smiled at my neighbours and friends, but in reality I was huddled in one room with my two children. I didn't want to lose face or appear to be struggling. I realised then that keeping up with the Joneses – trying to live a lifestyle that you think meets people's expectations of you – is a prison-sentence mentality. No one truly cares that much about what you wear and what you have – everyone has their own struggles and worries.

That was how my year had started. By the time October came around, and the water started to seep into the floorboards, my awareness, clarity and decision-making were totally out of sync. When I noticed that the floor had swelled, I ignored it. It came to the point that I would feel my socks getting wet but chose to deny something was wrong with my floor. My mind was elsewhere. I blocked it out of my mind until it was impossible to keep ignoring it.

Then one day my dad suggested I could claim for the repairs on my building insurance, something I had never even thought about. He suggested I call an assessor to see the likelihood of a successful claim. Thankfully the assessor came out and after surveying the damage, they put in a claim for me to get the floors replaced throughout the whole apartment. The insurance money was a godsend but went through my property management company, who deducted some of the money they were owed before I could even get my floors fixed.

From the insurance claim on the damage to my home, I received €10,000. The figure I ended up with was €4500 after the assessors received their fees and I had to pay back the property management my arrears. I could get the floor supplied and fitted for €4000 and then use the extra €500 towards debt.

(It was only in March 2019, right at the start of my debt-free journey, when I really learned that I could make my money stretch and get much more value for it with a little investigating and hard work. This first step in my journey set me on a path to so many revelations: where else could I save money? Getting my home fixed was a much-needed win for me, and I became obsessed with finding other necessary ways to make my money go further and bring myself and my family out of debt.)

In the past, I would've made decisions purely on the aesthetic basis; did I like the colour? What width was the timber? The price would've figured itself out. Then I would have experienced the stress of seeing if I was qualified to get that set amount on credit. Now however, I knew I needed to shop around, to do my research – to think carefully. If my dad couldn't do it, could I get a tradesman to do it for me? Could I afford that, along with the materials? Maybe laminate would do instead of semi-permanent, to make the budget work.

With the troubles of 2018 behind me, I knew I needed to do better, that my relationship with money was something that I needed to change, especially as I felt I had selfishly brought my children into this environment. It was time to rectify it. But where does one start?

I tried to declare insolvency, but that became complicated because I co-owned my apartment. So I looked to the internet and discovered this American lady called The Debt Kickin' Mom on YouTube. Finding her gave me hope. There she was, just another mammy working as a teacher and sharing her journey of overcoming huge amounts of debt and finding her way to financial security. I was transfixed, and would find every opportunity to tune into her. I couldn't believe what she was talking about in plain English. Budgeting, meal plans and everything that I would need to stay within my budget and bring myself out of debt. The best part was that many women like myself were tuning in every time she uploaded a video, to cheer her on. I watched so many videos that I knew I wanted that focus and accountability. In many ways, my prayers were answered. I knew I didn't have to do this all alone.

I sat down and began digging through my finances, which was the first time I realised I was €15,027 in debt. It was also when I started to understand just how crazy my outgoings were. I knew it was time to face this headon. So I went on Instagram with the same spirit as my mentor, The Debt Kickin' Mom, and shared that I was about to begin my debt-free journey – much to the bemusement of family and friends.

It wasn't a walk in the park. It was hard work, day in and day out. But it was an awakening, and even though I felt like an utter failure starting my debt-free journey, it was the best thing I've ever done. I managed to clear €15,027 in debt in one year, and yes, it was hard, and I wanted to give up, but I had to do it not just for me but for the women and men cheering me on every step of the way and starting their own roles in the debt-free community.

With this book I share simple advice and practical methods that I learned during my debt-free journey – advice and methods that I wish had been available to me back then. Unfortunately, money is not something we discuss with our friends and family; I think that's part of the problem. I hope this book is the starting point for discussing debt around the kitchen table.

I decided to train as a coach, adapting and learning to talk about money in a way that helps my clients become aware of their own behavioural pitfalls. This is something that I have not only studied but have been able to apply at every turn in my life. I am so proud to have helped so many people, and it is really important to me that you, the reader, might be able to benefit and learn from my mistakes and from what I've learned along the way. Hopefully, you'll be able to elevate yourself to not only survive, but thrive.

YOUR RELATIONSHIP
WITH MONEY

CHAPTER 1:

THE PSYCHOLOGY BEHIND OUR MONEY HABITS

Living with financial worries

According to a 2020 'How's Life' report from the Organisation for Economic Co-operation and Development (OECD), one in five European households currently find it difficult to make ends meet; one in eight live in relative income poverty; and one in three are **FINANCIALLY INSECURE**. This doesn't mean that they are poor or low-income, it means that, if there was a disruption in their earning power for as little as three months, they would find themselves defined as being in poverty.

Because poverty isn't just one-dimensional. It depends on specific social, economic, and political elements and comes in many different shapes and sizes:

Relative poverty concerns the government's definition and perspective of poverty based on that country's economic standard. It is based on a person's income, their number of dependants and what they can afford. It is the class of poverty most prevalent in wealthy, 'developed' countries.

Situational Poverty is where circumstances happen outside of your control, such as job loss or maybe a sudden health-related issue, and can lead a person to require social welfare. This tends to be a temporary state of poverty.

Consistent poverty relates to households on a low income and that are classed as being 'deprived'. Being deprived in Ireland generally means not being able to afford the following:

- heating
- two pairs of strong shoes
- a warm waterproof overcoat
- new (not second-hand) clothes
- meals with meat, chicken, fish (or the vegetarian equivalent) every second day and a roast joint (or its equivalent) once a week
- replacement of any worn-out furniture
- presents for family or friends at least once a year
- socialising with family or friends (for instance, for a drink or meal) once a month
- entertainment (not being able to have a morning, afternoon or evening out) once a fortnight

Remember, this applies to someone living this way permanently, not because they are making sustainable choices or trying to save money in their budget.

And financial worries are not limited to those on low incomes. People can earn high salaries and still struggle with money. I often get messages from people saying, 'Santis, we earn over €250,000 per year, yet we are still living payday to payday. How is that even possible?' I blame 'Keeping up with the Joneses'. Think about a doctor, for instance. They leave medical school (often up to their necks in student loans), start to make decent money but then **LIFE-STYLE INFLATION** occurs (when we upgrade our lifestyle as our income increases). They now have to be seen to live in a particular area, drive a specific car and socialise in certain circles, but this all comes at a cost.

I know bloggers and influencers who do the same. Suppose you work in fashion or beauty: some people assume it's essential to be wearing the latest of everything so the brand might notice you. But focusing on creating looks for your audience's benefit rather than exhibiting your own style leaves you tired and anxious. It is that Boss Babe or CEO lifestyle that has infiltrated society. We all know the saying, 'Fake it till you make it' – but so many fake it by acting (and spending!) like the person they think they should be, not the person they are.

And we've all heard of lottery winners who receive millions, only to lose it all (or, as I like to term it, *grow* broke). In cases like these, it's likely that the people involved had poor money-management skills to begin with, and their higher income just meant higher stakes – when they lost their grip on their finances, they had further to fall.

We all need a reset, big time. We live in a world where it is okay to show off your overconsumption in the hopes of being admired, but we need to encourage each other to spend within our means and not for the lifestyle we think we should be living.

Money does not make you happy, and it is not the be-all and end-all, but managing it well can help you on your way through life; and understanding it better can open the door to more, giving you access to options you might not have thought you had. I don't mean that we all need to start learning about advanced financial investments, such as playing the stock market, but it is important that we understand our learned behaviour towards money – and how to *un*learn it in order to develop it further. Having money can allow us to be comfortable, but, like all things, it must be approached mindfully.

We need to realise that the financial decisions we make now will affect our economic well-being in the future. We could talk about empowerment until the cows come home, but we need to act. To break the cycle, we need to become **FINANCIALLY LITERATE**. When we don't *know* any better, we can't *do* any better. Yet as a nation, we just don't talk about money; above religion and race it is the biggest taboo subject we have. So is it any wonder many of us struggle to handle our finances?

Now, it is essential that I highlight that you are not *bad* about money if your finances are looking a little unhealthy right now. It just means you need to be aware of the environments, triggers, saving and spending habits that may be keeping you in that unhealthy space.

Our environment and our attitude to money

First, you have to ask yourself *why* you think of money the way you do. Where did this idea come from? And it *is* an idea. From the moment we are born, we start to adapt to our environment: this can be our home life, the area we grew up in, the people we interacted with (at home or in school), basically anything we saw during our developing years. This creates in us a sort of genetic blueprint for how we think about most things, and money is no exception. By the time we are five years old we have already formed our **MONEY MINDSET**, and this not only informs our attitudes towards our own saving and spending habits, but our opinions on the finances of those we see around us.

And pay attention, because this is one of the big points I will keep coming back to in this book: we may not realise it, but we are conditioned to associate certain things with being accomplished, which all adds up to this idealised image of what constitutes wealth and success. There are things we see in others that allow us to make snap judgements on their social status: *how someone speaks* determines their net worth; *where someone lives* determines their net worth; *the way someone dresses* and the accessories they wear determines their status in life.

We assume that because someone has a well-paid job, they are financially secure. If we hear about someone rich having problems in their marriage or personal life, we are shocked because we assume being rich ends all problems. We have picked up on so many subtle cues and had so many conversations about money and they all have negatively or positively impacted our financial wellbeing.

As a money-mindset coach I have collaborated with many clients, and when I ask them to explain their behaviours around money, I tend to hear the same sort of things time and again:

- None of my family has ever been good with money.
- I am from a line of spenders.
- I am from a working-class background.
- I don't want to become a snob if I start earning more money.
- Everyone I know gets credit union loans for holidays.
- In one hand, out the other.
- Rich people are born with money.

Now, if I am honest, these are the same sort of things I used to say before I decided to become accountable for my finances. I come from a working-class family. I have lived through times of extreme financial worry, and for years I just accepted that this was the way things would be as that was how they had always been. I wanted more in life, but I was afraid to say my dreams out loud because they felt unattainable: I didn't think I could start my own business because I thought that only people from privilege could be entrepreneurs. So I filled the void by buying things. Whatever it took to make me feel like I was enough, that I was successful. I was impulsive and often acquired things for the wrong reason; I believed that if I *looked* the part, then I would *feel* the part.

But it was only ever a front to mask how things really were, and I felt that things would never change.

We tend to fall back on our old familiar excuses, and sometimes it's comforting to think that things are the way they are because that's the way they have always been. That's certainly how I felt. But that kind of thinking can lead to us getting stuck, making the same mistakes over and over again.

And the truth is, we don't need to *stay* stuck. Instead of saying to ourselves, 'I am just not good with money,' we must learn to say, 'So how do we fix this?' And instead of teaching the next generation our old excuses, we should try to develop a home environment in which children are encouraged to talk openly about money: one that gets them interested in the household budget and shows them the power of creating good saving habits. We need to show them that **MONEY IS A TOOL**.

In the same way we help our children learn how to ride a bike, we need to educate them to understand the power of good money habits (I wish I could have advised my younger self to save a little at a time, so that the Santis in her thirties could be thankful to the Santis in her twenties). Education plays such a big role in all of this. I'm sure that, growing up, many of us would have heard our parents say things like, 'There's not enough money for that,' and while I don't see anything wrong with being honest, we need to start having *positive* conversations around money. When my children are getting a treat, I'll always say, 'Let me get the money that I saved for that,' because this leads to a positive association with saving money.

We need to *normalise* talking about money. It is unbelievable to think Ireland stands still every October to listen to the minister of finance announce the country's annual budget. We watch and wait to see how it affects us personally. Then, we go about our lives with a sigh instead of applying those changes to our finances.

I genuinely see the need to bring home every bit of news we hear that can affect us financially. That's why talking about money should be normalised – we should be inquisitive about, and adapt to, the information that is out there, applying what we learn to our own circumstances.

Money personality types

As I always say, *it is only with awareness that change can begin*. And the best place to start is to take a step back and figure out what kind of relationship you currently have with money; to determine your **MONEY PERSONALITY TYPE**.

Have a read through the following and see which one you most identify with:

The Constant Earner: You like to make money – for you, it is a constant obsession. You love to be seen and noted for being financially successful. Because of this, you are likely to be a high achiever in other aspects of your life too.

The Spender: You tend to spend money as soon as it comes in. You love the reward of the purchase as it offers instant gratification. You enjoy looking after the people around you and treating them to gifts. You are an emotional spender and would not let debt deter you when it comes to your spending habits. You don't really budget, and it is only when something dramatic happens that you might even notice that you have a problem.

The Risk-taker: You get bored when taking things slowly and steadily and would rather have no money than not be able to take part in high-risk ways of accumulating it. You get a thrill from taking chances and enjoy taking risks with your finances. You love to win, but the losses can get to you as the risks are never fully thought out. Most likely, you work in a high-risk job.

The Free Spirit: You think the world would be a nicer place if everyone just shared what they had. You like to give back to the community and often raise or donate money, distributing it to people in need.

The Worrier-Collector: For you, having money provides the ultimate security. You fear that you might lose your money at any time, therefore you are uncomfortable spending it and feel that you have to keep stacking up the cash, but for no tangible outcome. You are hyper-aware of the price of things, and are always on the lookout for bargains. You wouldn't be caught dead making random purchases. You may have grown up in an environment where money was tight, so you feel the need to be frugal.

The Worrier-Spender: You are good at saving money but are tempted from time to time to be a spendthrift. When you do splurge, it is rarely on things you need, as you are more of an emotional spender. Your expenses are often unplanned.

The Oblivious: Money does not drive you, and you tend to spend a lot of it on your passion, which might be your hobby or your job. You do not work to live but live to work; obsessed with work simply because it is there. Most likely you come from a background where money was plentiful, and you'll admit to not being very financially literate, preferring to delegate money matters to someone else.

So, what type of money personality are you? Which would you prefer to be?

Perhaps you're thinking, *Well, I don't want to be any of these!* And you'd be right: too much of any one thing can be terrible, but a little bit of everything gives balance. For instance, it may sound great on paper to be an **Oblivious** (where money is plentiful and someone else takes care of all your financial paperwork!) but if you have zero knowledge of essential financial tools, you may experience intense anxiety or worry if something should go wrong. Or maybe you know a **Risk-taker** who always seems to strike it lucky with their endeavours, and you envy them their success; this personality trait can also be prevalent in those with gambling addictions. Having worked in a betting shop for seventeen years, I am all too familiar with this type of spender, and while there is nothing wrong with taking risks now and again, everything must balance and you will lose at some point. Too much of everything becomes problematic.

Ideally, you should aim to find the middle ground between all of these personalities, taking the best traits from each and incorporating them into your own money mindset.

But no matter which Money Personality you see yourself as having, your goal should be to get to a place of **FINANCIAL WELLNESS**.

What is financial wellness?

Financial wellness is a buzzword right now. There are many institutions out there who aim to provide advice on your financial health, to help you make somewhat informed decisions around personal finances. But please, do your research and make sure that you understand what it would mean for *you* to be financially well. Knowledge is power!

Let's face it, we need money. It is the currency of today's society. It facilitates most of our basic needs and the things we need to live a decent life. *But for so long, society has told us that our self-worth equates to our net worth*, and that is one of the reasons why there is so much shame around money.

Now, it is only natural that our finances will occupy our thoughts some of the time. But to be financially well, you need to be in a position where thinking about money does not become part of your day-to-day life; where it does not take the lead role in your decision-making.

Like any well-being journey, the key here is **AWARENESS**. In order to get to a place of financial well-being we need to understand what it means to be financially *un*well. Here are some key signs:

- You don't have a financial plan – you never know what's going on with your money.
- You rely on credit to live day-to-day.
- You avoid conversations about money and feel anxious at the mention of unforeseen costs.
- You live in fear that you might lose your source of income, which would spell disaster.
- You are constantly worrying about money, which in turn affects other parts of your well-being. You have no appetite, can't sleep and have zero motivation to get things done.
- You feel intimidated about budgeting and constantly ask yourself, 'Where would I start?'
- You don't have an emergency fund and view having one as impossible. You know that you are not prepared for any last-minute or unforeseen expenditure.

Does any of this sound familiar? Maybe what you are doing, like so many others, is firefighting when it comes to your finances, facing problem after problem, money worry after money worry, barely resolving one issue before another comes along. You try to avoid talking and thinking about money because these thoughts leave you feeling inadequate. But by doing that, you are devaluing yourself and your future. *You deserve peace of mind; you deserve to value your future.* You deserve to set goals around your wildest dreams and work towards them; goals that align with who you want to be, and what you want to do with your time here on earth.

Emotional preparation for the road ahead

Now, if you're holding a copy of this book, then it's likely that you've already made the decision to move towards a more financially healthy state. Deadly – let's keep it going! Taking that first step is always the hardest part. But as we all know, the only way to make a major life change, and stick to it, is to really want it, and like all worthwhile things it will take some time, effort and practice to get there.

There will be many obstacles and challenges before you get to the end of your journey and without a doubt, the biggest battle will be with yourself. Here are some tips to overcome any self-sabotaging thoughts that may come up:

- Words have meaning, so choose carefully how you speak to yourself and others about money. I used to look in the mirror and tell myself I was good with money, that I would be debt free.
- Avoid those with only negative things to say about your journey. If they are not going to help you get to your destination, then they do not get an input.
- Take some time for reflection. I reflected every single day, week and month on how far I had come on my journey. It helped keep me motivated.
- Embrace accountability. I used to go on to Instagram and share how much I'd paid off every single week.
- Find a mentor – seek help and advice from people you genuinely admire. I looked to others who had done what I was trying to do, but instead of comparing myself to them, I took in every tip and trick they shared and applied it to my journey.
- Get comfortable with being uncomfortable. Being uncomfortable means growth: when you are not challenged, you are not growing.
- Meditate, do breathing work and/or journaling. I am creative, so it was vital for me to find a calm moment in the day to get some of my thoughts out of my head.
- Make time. We all have the same hours in our days. I worked full time and was a single mother of two young children – how was I to find the time for planning, budgeting and meditating? The answer? I woke up at 5 a.m. when I needed to have some quiet time.

- Exercise. As I said, I was time-poor, so it was tempting to skip this step. Instead I started skipping and walking to work and back when I had the opportunity, in order to get my exercise in and save money.

You are committing to this financial wellness journey because you know that it can get you to a stronger, more organised position in life. Make no mistake, this is a lifestyle change – one that is wonderful and liberating and absolutely worth it, but a lifestyle change all the same. You want to make sure that it is as easy and sustainable as possible, and to do that, you need to make sure that you are taking care of yourself.

Identifying your triggers

It's also important that you be mindful of your **TRIGGERS** – those habits of yours that keep causing you to spend. And the truth is that we spend money for a myriad of reasons, the most straightforward being that we simply need the item (food, clothing, shelter). But with the constant exposure to, and push/pull of, consumerism and consumption – the 'buy this, buy that' of modern living – a lot of us have become emotional spenders. We buy things that we don't need, whether to help us portray a certain image to the world, or because we want to be part of the crowd, or we have a fear of missing out. Some people spend out of boredom, or because they get instant gratification from it.

I genuinely think that people forget that the first port of call to fixing anything is usually internal. Very rarely do we *need* to buy anything, but we get caught up in the over-consumerism machine. Take clothes, for example: we follow a trend, and soon have to keep up with many trends. We are told what's in fashion, so we buy what's in fashion. Then the season changes, and it's another trend that we follow. It is a cycle and what maybe starts with clothes leads to decor or even the car you choose to drive. Unfortunately, we are all victims of this – we start to lose ourselves and, therefore, our originality. I cringe with sadness when I hear people (most frequently, young girls) say, 'I can't wear that outfit again as there was a picture of me wearing it on social media.' We don't have favourite outfits any more, we have the latest trend.

We are in a culture where we get caught up in the hamster wheel of consumerism. Everywhere we look, we are being sold something – and, look, I don't have a problem with ads or the marketing department of any firm, I'm just aware of the excellent work they do. Getting you to consume is a huge business. Some influencers fabricate a perfect life so you can buy into it, even though you know that such a thing doesn't exist. It is a ploy to sell you products; to buy your way into coexisting in their world. But unfortunately most consumers are not aware of the issue, and the lack of awareness contributes to most problems. So if you are not mindful of how your spending habits are triggered, how do you limit them?

What you need to do is find *your* reason for over-spending; work out what your triggers are. I suggest keeping a journal – use it to make a note of your spending habits and, any time you are triggered to spend, ask yourself these questions:

- What happened?
- What was my mood leading up to it?
- How do I feel after spending?

If you find that going to certain places or meeting with certain people encourages you to spend, then do your best to avoid them . . . or at least minimise your exposure to them!

In my case, I realised though my journaling that I would overspend when I was feeling emotional: the days coming up to my period; after a bad day in work; one of those days where my children had pushed me to my limits; or as a reward for doing something new. Spending on these occasions sent my endorphins alight, and that feeling was a huge rush. It was addictive. But now, when I start to feel a certain way, I know I need to avoid going online. Instead I will go for a walk, read a book, engage in a hobby, meet friends . . . anything to make sure I avoid temptation.

It is essential that we understand that there are **EMOTIONS** present in how we approach money, and getting people to realise that is a core part of my money mentoring.

For the most part, people tend to focus on our intellectual intelligence (what we'll call our **IQ**) without understanding the emotional intelligence (our **EQ**) behind it, yet our EQ informs so much of what we do. For example, if you looked at money and budgeting from a purely IQ-led standpoint, you would memorise the tips and budgeting techniques and walk away knowing the concepts behind how to budget.

But if you add EQ to the mix, you can learn how to identify the emotions attached to budgeting and money, which will, in turn, help you to:

- identify and control your triggers;
- figure out how these relate to you and to others;
- recognise how this makes you feel; and
- realise how being good with your money makes you feel.

Just because we know what to do, does not always mean we do it. I have accountants that come to me for budgeting tips – being smart, or even working in a certain environment, does not guarantee successful money management. Your brain needs to connect with your heart and your gut when budgeting.

When we break it down, we all know the numbers. We just need to understand why making them work for us is crucial. We need to work towards and maintain a contented, happy life. And that is what we are going to be looking at in the next few chapters. I want you to walk away from reading this book with all the practical information you will need to keep you moving in the right direction.

Food for thought – women, finance and careers.

Awareness is one of the essential tools for problem-solving, and I think the role women play in personal and household finances should be highlighted so that we can address some of the major issues we all face with our money today.

Ladies, we are in an era of total reformation. Why? Women are not only marching to fight for their rights to be treated as equals in society and at home, but also for recognition of the work we do; we are in the era of female empowerment. So how are our finances affected by this?

Are we earning more?

Are we facing new challenges?

Are we balancing motherhood and working in a more demanding environment than ever?

So many women have walked before us and fought for equal rights. They planted seeds so that we might face the sun. But the funny thing with history is that it leaves scars and trauma as well as progress. My hope for this book is that you come away feeling empowered, knowing your worth and ultimately understanding the importance of standing in your financial power. I hope that I can help to shed light on the financial pitfalls laid out for us (and sometimes *by* us). We have made much progress, but we're still a long way off.

In school, some of us were taught home economics, but we should all have been learning about personal finance in a relatable way, especially those of us who didn't get much of an education about money at home. Thankfully, there are more resources than ever now for us to get educated about managing our money and give ourselves the tools to improve our financial situations. Time after time, I have had women reaching out to me from many different circumstances, and in offering them advice, I realised that it doesn't take much to make a difference. So, here I am, a single mother who talks about money, and I've seen first-hand the impact that has had on other women, helping them towards financial wellness.

As women we have new and growing opportunities to not only earn at the higher tiers and learn how to manage our money effectively, but also to thrive with our money. Unfortunately, we all have many misconceptions and attitudes regarding money. I wonder, are you as guilty as I am and have been? For me, it has often been almost impossible to imagine myself earning much money, because I haven't seen many people like me in high-powered roles here in Ireland. I always say that **SEEING IS BEING** so if we don't see, it's impossible to imagine that we can be.

As a black woman who grew up in a working-class house, it's sometimes impossible for me to even get my head around the idea that certain levels of success are possible.

It is unusual to hear a woman speak about money outside home economics and managing money at home. And although I am a personal finance enthusiast – which starts at home – I know that I will move on to bigger things as I move through life. Partly because I feel a personal responsibility to do so, and it's up to me to show my nieces, women and women of colour that it's time to unlearn the negative patterns and behaviours that were drilled into us. My problem is that I, like so many people, have been told through movies, social media and marketing companies that women are not good with money. We are deemed either frivolous or spend-thrifts. The standards set for women and men are still very different: while our male counterparts are sharing tips on investing, we are still told to learn how to manage our homes.

The more I deep-dived into financial education, the more I realised that the odds are stacked against us from the beginning. Historically, women were seen as commodities, things to be sold as bartering tools used to unite families. We were trophies or carriers of heirs. We were second to men; unfortunately, we still live in many ways with the imprint of these traditions. It almost feels that we have been groomed from an early age to play the supporting role of the nurturer, subservient, the role of being the little woman rather than being equal. We're told it's good to be obedient and to do as you're told. And this is something that is continued throughout adulthood. So this creates the need to please and make sure that everybody around us is happy, even if it means putting ourselves second. It's a wonder that women have come as far as they have in society.

If you are an ambitious woman, words like 'ruthless' and 'cold' are easily thrown our way when our male counterparts are viewed as focused and great leaders. We associate a strong man as an alpha, a top earner, a leader, but a woman in the same position is deemed selfish and cold. Thankfully, the world is changing, and we must be seen as more than the nurturers of the home. How many of us berate ourselves with such debilitating self-criticism that it becomes nearly impossible to ask for a pay rise? Never mind going for promotions. We can't be treated with the respect we've earned in the workplace after having a child. It doesn't matter how long you've worked for the company or how hard you've worked to get to your position. When you have a child, you become of less value to your employer. Why is this?

So many women have seen that and have had to give up their full-time jobs, no matter how good they were at them, because it became more critical for them to focus on their children, which meant that they felt they could no longer give the same amount of time and energy to their employers. If I didn't see this first-hand, I probably would never talk about it, but this is something that happens, and many women go through this. This is something our male counterparts would never have to deal with. We are so programmed to please that we put ourselves second to do so. When you do things for other people, especially in the workplace, with little or no benefit to yourself, you sacrifice doing those things that can benefit you and your career.

We aim to please, and we aim to be the best at everything. But often, instead of sharing the household and child-rearing responsibility equally between us and our partner – if we have one – we take it all on ourselves.

As I said before, I don't see a lot of black females in the situation that I am trying to get into, and so in some ways I feel an added pressure now, to be an example of excellence. And part of this is growing my financial awareness and my knowledge around how to manage my money, as I truly feel that having control over my money gives me control over my choices, and proper financial freedom would give me the greatest control. Some of these choices will mean coming up against assumptions about our role as women, which is something I'm keen we push back against, so that we can thrive both at home and in our careers – which in turn will allow us to thrive with our money. I suggested to my mother that when I reached a certain threshold in my career, I would get someone to clean the house for me: that way I could focus on my family when I got home from work. The first response I got was, as expected, 'Sure you can always find time to clean your house.' This made me think that if I were the man making the same decision, no one would look twice at me. This did give me much food for thought, and it also told me that sometimes the biggest problem for women succeeding and accelerating their growth is looking to justify their decisions in the minds of others. Because as women we have to focus on so many different things with equal levels of care, it can often feel impossible to get to the height of our careers – even though we know we have the ability to do so.

So why is this so important, and what does it have to do with your money? There is a hidden cost financially for women when having children as our careers very often take a backseat, leading to delays in career progression, and by extension to increases in our income. I know so many women who have given up work just because their job was not flexible enough to enable them to adapt to both parenthood and work. I've worked for several organisations, and not once have I heard of a situation like this where the employee was male.

We women have historically been on the back foot when it came to money, and while things are obviously changing in positive ways, there is still a lingering belief that women aren't good with money. I am determined to counter that belief – and to help other women realise that there is huge freedom in having control over your own finances. Yes, we are no longer in an era where women stay at home while men go out to work (it's worth remembering that the Marriage Bar, which determined that no married women were able to be employed, was only abolished in Ireland in 1977!) but it's undeniable that we still battle against biases and disadvantages both in the workplace and in society. I believe that one of the best ways of combating these issues is to begin by securing our financial freedom, which then gives us the opportunity to have control of what choices we make.

Mentor's Notes
- Understand the environment from which your relationship to money is formed.
- Do we know who influences us on our journey to spending money?
- Our emotional intelligence (EQ) is the key to implementing our financial overhaul.

CHAPTER 2:

TAKING STOCK OF YOUR FINANCES

So now that we've had a look at the psychology behind our spending and attitudes to money in general, it's time to pull up our socks, roll up our sleeves, and get stuck in! You know where you want to be, and I want to help you get there.

This chapter will cover those all-important steps that are necessary at the start of any road to financial wellness.

Generate a financial plan

I am often asked what advice I would give to my younger self, based on the knowledge I now have, and my answer is always the same: I would tell myself to create a financial plan.

Never underestimate the importance of having a healthy financial plan! Creating one should be the first step you take, even if it's just something you have scribbled on a scrap of paper. And it can be as simple or as complicated as you like, so long as it takes note of:

- your current money situation;
- your long-term monetary goal and your *why*;
- the strategies you can (and will!) implement to achieve that goal.

When you don't have a plan for your life, then you end up being at the mercy of what someone else has planned for you. This applies to your financial plan also. If I know that in ten years' time I will want to have a mortgage or I will want to have children, then I also know that right now I need to be saving towards it. I'm less likely to get a credit union loan for frivolous things. And instead, it might make more sense for me to put a little bit of my money away into a savings account for my house or my future children. When you create a plan for what's to come it makes you more inclined to think of all of your short-term actions as being part of an overall picture.

It also saves you money. If you're somebody who is reading the news and see that house prices are going up, you may decide to start saving for your house right now so you can get on the property ladder. Otherwise, you risk making a rash decision based on external advice and you could miss out on the chances of getting the best deal, the best interest rate. If you have a financial plan, this could be something that you study or investigate along the way. I bought my first home because I didn't want to travel to Australia. That is no premise for making such a long-term commitment.

This will help you to make sure that you're saving in the best account; to wait until there is a dip in the market or until it stabilises; it allows you to accumulate compound interest by investing now, because by planning ahead you have more time for your money to mature. And you will absolutely understand what it takes to have a mortgage, save for a mortgage, and get the best deal that the bank has on offer.

What is a financial plan?

Writing a financial plan might be the best thing you can do to secure your financial future. Unfortunately, a lot of us put it off because we assume that it's back-breaking work; to be able to do so, many people seem to think they need professional help. However, that is not really the case – making a financial plan can be very straightforward.

A financial plan is a working tool that allows you to assess your current financial position in relation to your financial goals. First, you must know what you want to get out of a financial plan. What are your objectives? Writing up and maintaining an effective financial plan is not a one-time task but an ongoing process – your financial plan changes with your circumstances.

A financial plan is tailored for the individual around one key question: **WHY IS MONEY IMPORTANT TO YOU?** If money matters to you because of security, then the next question to ask is what do you need to do to build that security. If money is important to you so that you can build generational wealth, what actions do you need to take to get the ball rolling? The critical thing is that you're honest with yourself when answering this question. Because ultimately, we want to build *your* financial plan for *your* future.

There are a few key steps when it comes to beginning your financial plan:

- Understand and establish your goals. What are you planning for?
- Have a good look at your current financial situation. There is no point in investing if you're barely able to pay your mortgage. Bring together all information – incomings and outgoings – that make up your current financial situation.
- Be prepared to act and to be flexible in order to implement your plan and make changes as needed. By constantly reviewing your finances, you can adapt to whatever change is coming down the line. I always think it's not a step back; it's a delay.

So how does a financial plan differ from a budget? With a budget, you record your income and expenses regularly, which enables you to reach your short-term goals, without looking too far into the future. With a financial plan, you track your overall progress towards your goals on a regular basis, always with an eye on the future. A budget is a crucial part of the strategy to implement your long-term plan, but it is just one part. The financial plan is the bigger picture.

With a financial plan, you're considering your whole financial future:

- Are you able to afford kids?
- Are you prepared for retirement?
- Do you want to build wealth?
- How are you going to live the life of your dreams?
- What do you want your life to be like?
- What kind of job do you need to implement this lifestyle you're planning?
- Reviewing and including your partner when making a financial plan is also essential.

If you don't know your goals for the future, that's okay, but it can be difficult to create a plan for that. However, I do now believe that if I had a financial plan years ago, before I began my cycle of debt, I would currently be in a much better financial position. What's important to remember with all of this is that you have to be realistic with your financial goals. Some things in life are unpredictable.

My financial plan is now a staple in my life and reassures me when things don't go exactly the way I'd like them to go in the time frame that I had planned. It also gives me purpose when I'm doing my budget. Budgeting can be repetitive, but when you can see **THE BIGGER PICTURE** and how you're working towards it each month, you'll understand why you're doing it.

Here is an example of how I write my financial plan, where at the bottom A – B = net worth:

Income (A1)	Expenses (B1)
Monthly income after tax (the money that reaches you) and every other source of income, such as child maintenance.	Monthly expenses – utilities, mortgage repayments.
Income total:	**Expenses total:**
Assets (A2)	**Debts (B2)**
Your assets such as your home, car, savings, shares – you need to determine how much they are worth. You might need a professional financial planner to wowrk out some of these.	Debts – personal loans, credit cards, other forms of personal debt.
Assets total:	**Debts total:**
Overall total:	Overall total:
Income and assets minus expenses and debts =	

Knowing your net worth means that you have a clearer sense of your current financial position. It might end up in a surplus or deficit, but it will be a useful starting point. This is where your budget comes in handy because if you're in a deficit, your budget tells you where you need to reduce your spending. To help get the clearest picture from your financial plan, it's worth closely tracking your spending. Knowing where you stand might also give you the confidence to reach out to creditors and lending institutions rather than hiding from them. When I didn't know what was going on with my finances, it heightened my anxiety around money. However, once I knew, I was able to make a positive move forward.

One thing I did immediately after creating my first financial plan, for example, was to set up a life insurance policy and a will for my children. It was something I had never thought about but became a high priority in my life at that point, and the clarity I got from my plan helped me make that realisation. As I refer back to my plan, I constantly ask myself what money means to me and what I want from my money. Set yourself a goal and a *why*.

The most important part of any financial plan is your **GOAL**. Your goal will become your energy source. It will be the driving force that keeps you going on your money management mission. So set clear goals, outlining what it is you want to gain from this budgeting experience.

You also need to be very clear about your **WHY** – why have you chosen this particular goal? And it can be anything, big or small, so long as it is enough to keep you going when things get tough.

Goal: To be debt free   **Why?** I want to work less/choose my own path

Goal: Go on an exotic holiday   **Why?** It has always been my dream to see the world

Goal: Have my own house   **Why?** To set down roots for my children

Goal: To be financially literate **Why?** I want to make my
money work best for me

Goal: Create a long-term saving plan **Why?** I want to
future-proof my finances for my children

Goal: To prepare for my future **Why?** I don't want to worry
about money in the future

Goal: Escape financial abuse **Why?** To step into my power
and take ownership of my life

Finding your *why* should nearly move you to tears because
you have hit upon something that fully aligns with your values
and what is important to you.

For example, when I started my own money wellness
journey, my *why* was simple: I was desperate to clear my
debts. I wanted to be present, and grateful to be in my
children's lives. It was my driving force for my debt pay-off,
and it gave me so much hope. The emotions associated with
being debt-free were so strong that every time I picked up
my budget and saw my progress, I would well up. I would
stay up late at night looking up ways to cut costs around
the house. It felt like a pull, week in, week out, to make
conscious decisions that would allow me to pay extra towards
my debt.

And whenever I felt my resolve slipping, whenever I was
tempted to stop, I would open the door to my kids' room
and just seeing them sleeping there would remind me what
it was all for. My *why* was huge, and nothing or no one
would get in the way of it. Eliza and Louis deserved better
than only having half of me. So, I would go back to my

laptop and look up fun, cheap things we could do as a family (I loved going on trips to the park and hearing my inquisitive children ask questions about the changing colours of the trees). I took pride in taking action; this consistency is self-love.

Your *why* needs to be huge, people, because it is not just a pipe dream; it needs to be big enough to overcome any obstacles that might try to mess with your momentum.

And maintaining momentum is key to any lifestyle change. No matter what your goals may be, they are only achievable if you keep at them. One of the tricks to this is breaking your goals down into achievable milestones over a specific period. It may not be possible to save enough for a home deposit in just one year, but you can set yourself manageable targets instead. How much do you want to have saved in six months? In a year? In two years? A little pressure is good, but not too much. So adjust the time and the target to suit your circumstances.

And you can adjust your goals and your *whys* too. A financial plan is not something you should do just once: as your circumstances change, and you grow in confidence, you may find that it changes and evolves right along with you.

When I paid off my debt, my goals changed. As I had worked towards being debt-free, I received so many messages from people who associated money, and debt in particular, with shame. I was saddened by this, but I was also angry as I realised just how huge this problem was. I wanted to get people to start talking about money in a healthy, positive way – it became my new goal. So I went onto radio stations,

I offered to write pieces in magazines for free, I set up a YouTube channel, I did take-overs on prominent social-media channels and pages. These all made me so uncomfortable as I was doing so many things outside of my comfort zone – approaching people I didn't know, for example, which often ended in rejection; putting myself out there for ridicule; talking about my insecurities and things that most people were uncomfortable hearing about – but energy comes with purpose.

I started seeing more people talking about money after that, and so my goals changed again – I decided I wanted to normalise budgeting, and I set my mind to getting one million people to budget. This is a very personal goal that I am sharing with you, because Santis of a few years ago would not have dreamt of even doing a budget. But my *why* was so emotionally charged that it fuelled me to step outside of my comfort zone and make this happen. So:

- I created a budget planner;
- I opened an online shop where I sell budgeting products;
- I started to coach families on how to manage their finances.

Then the radio stations and magazines started coming to me. I was co-presenter on *The Price of Everything,* a prime-time show on RTÉ, I decided to write this book and I have now, along with my business partner Grainne McNamee, set up The Budget Mindset Club Limited, a service that provides courses on a variety of money-related topics, with weekly live motivational coaching around progress, hot topics and accountability. And this was all because I had identified my goal (to help as many people as I possibly can) and, most importantly, my *why* (to change the mindset around money in Ireland), which aligned with my personal value of sharing knowledge.

Having your *why* is the emotional back up that your intellect needs.

Give yourself a money NCT

Your next step is to get yourself organised. Take stock of your income and expenditure, and generally give yourself a **MONEY NCT**. You *need* to know where your money is going. You want to see the full picture, the pattern behind your spending habits, so be prepared for an eye-opening journey. If you constantly find yourself with zero money with more than a week/fortnight/month to go before payday, you are about to find out why.

First, you should **start religiously tracking your casual spending with pen and paper**. You need to follow your spending to see your habits with money. Keep those receipts in a safe place so you can review them. This is a worthwhile task as it will put you face to face with your money habits.

Next, you need to **examine all your bank, credit card and financial statements** with a fine-tooth comb. Make sure you have a clear and defined list of what's coming in – salary, benefits, money made from mystery shopping or surveys – and what's going out. Take the time to be thorough, and make sure you understand and make note of the amount; when the transaction occurred; and what exactly it was for. You need full transparency – remember, awareness brings growth – so, if you do not understand a transaction, take your time and investigate. Ring that bank, stay on hold, go through your receipts, do whatever it takes.

Take particular note of any debts you may have:

- Do you have an overdraft?
- Do you have a higher purchase agreement?
- Do you have any outstanding credit card payments?
- If you owe a friend or family member money, you are now indebted to them, so their names with the amount should also appear on the list.

Have you started paying these back? If so, how much do you regularly pay? Debt is presented to us in all shapes and sizes, and it is stressful to manage, so acquiring it should never be your first option. Just remember this: borrowers are slaves to the lender and paying off a debt takes focus and dedication.

So create a debt list:

- How much do you owe?
- Who do you owe?
- What is your timeline to repay this loan?
- Will you be penalised for paying it back early?
- How is your interest calculated?

Don't get me wrong, I don't think all debt is bad – a mortgage is a prime example of good debt, and so too are credit cards. Yes, you read that right – credit cards can offer good debt. If managed correctly (by which I mean the balance is paid off every month, and not just the minimum repayments) then using a credit card is a great way to improve your credit rating.

Some of the most common types of debts are from:

- *Family and friends*: These are emotionally taxing and could be really bad for your personal relationships. Once you owe somebody money, then you are inclined to act differently around them.
- *Zero interest credit offers:* Nothing in this life is free. Miss or get behind on payments, and this becomes a high-interest loan.
- *Hire purchase:* You don't own the item (whether a new car, sofa or phone) until it is paid for in full, plus it will cost more overall.
- *Loan sharks:* These thrive on low-income families that have bad credit and feel they have nowhere else to turn.
- *Payday loans:* These are unsecured loans taken for a short period of time and usually have a colossal level of interest attached. It is difficult to clear these loans.
- *Credit union:* Often seen as the banks of the community, I discuss the benefits and pitfalls of these in Chapter 8.
- *Store cards:* a credit card for one particular store.

- *Mortgage*
- *Student loans:* low-interest loans given to students to supplement their fees/accommodations whilst in college. Some countries have a huge student loan problem but thankfully, in Ireland student loans have no hidden charges and the repayment structure is suited towards the borrower.

I think it's important that I highlight the role of a bank here as most of our debts are held by institutions and banks. It's important that we know who they are and how they make their money. Banks cost a lot to run (think about the staff, the security, all that software) and you might assume that they make money from their service charges, but that is not the case. Banks make their money by selling financial services such as loans, overdrafts, mortgages, credit cards and so on. These products all cost the consumer money through, for instance, the interest rates charged on each.

At the end of the day, a bank is a business. So this sense of loyalty that we have towards *them* can mean that we end up being disloyal to the business of managing our home and our personal finances. So remember:

- Is important to make sure that you have the best possible account out there. So make sure you shop around and get the best rates.
- Make sure you understand *your* needs. Check in with your financial plan and focus on getting what you want from your money.

• Create new habits and turn the cycle of paying debts into savings.

The reason why it's so important to do a money NCT is to make sure that you don't continue to build debt. It's important that you stop and assess where you are *right now*. If you stay in debt, if you keep borrowing money, or even if you pay your debt back nice and slowly (paying those extra fees and interest), you will make the banking institutions very happy. It doesn't really make any sense, does it? To always have a portion of your income eaten up by paying your debt?

Being in debt is the single most important threat to your financial freedom.

Now that you have a comprehensive list of all your incomings and outgoings, you need to categorise whether those expenses are **VARIABLE** or **FIXED**.

Variable expenses are outgoings in which the amount can change from one week to another, sometimes higher and sometimes lower. These are usually for things we *want* rather than *need* – for instance, the amount you spend on eating out – but it can also include necessities, like your weekly food budget. Loans like your mortgage can be a variable expense also.

Fixed expenses are what I like to call long-term expenses; those outgoings for which the amount does not change – for instance, your insurance, phone bill and so on. A fixed expense is usually a basic need, but it can also include things like streaming services and subscriptions.

I tend not to use the term 'fixed', however. The reason for this is psychological as it implies permanence – but nothing is permanent. A perfect example of this is my mortgage repayment. Every month I pay €1,165 into my mortgage account. I earn €500 per week, so I repeatedly see that the word 'fixed' applies to a little over half of my expenses. It can make you feel just that: fixed. Yes, this is an outgoing that is non-negotiable, but now I take students in when I can to help with that payment, and I am looking to move to somewhere with more space and a lower price tag. My mortgage is a *priority*, but nothing has to be fixed unless you want it to be.

On the other hand, I found some of my everyday expenses hard to swallow: how did getting a taxi twice a week for work add up to over €1,000 a year? That is a huge price to pay to avoid being late! And that coffee and muffin deal I was getting 2–3 days a week at €3 a pop? That was costing me over €458 per year. Those two expenses alone could have paid for a monthly mortgage repayment. Although I know everybody blames coffee when it comes to looking at how we spend, it is genuinely the small habits that we need to look to change first. Getting up that little bit earlier to ensure you arrive to work on time – and even with enough time to spare to make a coffee in the canteen or kitchen – can save you so much money.

No matter how shocked you might feel after seeing your spending habits, please keep going. You are now on the way to bossing your money, but first comes a bit of clarity and awareness. So often our mind will make everything appear more than it is. Get it out of your head and down on paper. You won't regret it.

Cut down on your spending

Thanks to your money NCT, you should now have a crystal-clear picture of exactly where your money has been going. It can be intimidating, yes, but it is also incredibly liberating: you now have in front of you a set of data that you can use to really get your finances into shape.

For me, one of the most useful outcomes of doing the NCT is that it makes us more mindful of what we actually want to be spending our money on. Even if you are financially well, I am sure that there are one or two shockers on that list, and culling any unnecessary spending – things that, once you weigh them up, aren't really worth the cost, and maybe aren't even what you want – is a great way to kick-start your new, healthier approach to money.

So my advice is to take your list and eliminate as many online and digital spending habits as you can find.

Start by **checking for subscriptions and memberships that you pay for but do not use.** If you want to find a quick way to save money, this is one of the simplest. Many companies offer free trials before a subscription starts. It is a clever way of luring us in and is a known tactic for increasing customer sales. It shows that companies are confident in their products, and it sets a tone of trust between us (the consumer) and the respective company. But what if, on the week of Black Friday, you sign up to multiple offers, deciding that you want to try before you buy. Next thing you know, the seven days are up, the free trial is over and there you are, roped into contract for a year because you didn't cancel in time and had to hand over your payment details to avail of the free trial. (My tip for this is to set an alarm on your phone to remind you to cancel.) Unused subscriptions are like having a cup with a tiny hole in the bottom. The liquid is just dripping out, your hand feels wet, but you don't know where it's coming from. So let's seal that leak!

Once you've started the ball rolling and you've cut out obvious unwanted spends, you may find that you want take it further. My suggestion is that you should **create a *want* or *need* checklist.** Go through your list of expenditures and list each one as a want or a need. Then take the list of wants and really think about whether each one is worth enough to you to stay on your list. Do you really want to keep paying for it? And remember balance is essential in life, so if your needs outweigh your wants, and your want is something you truly desire, then keep it.

And now that you have whittled down your outgoings list as much as you can, you'll want to prevent yourself from adding to it again.

For me, one of the simplest, most effective and *practical* ways to do this is to make it as difficult as possible for yourself to spend in the first place. We live in a world in which it is much too easy to buy things: technology has made the ability to make purchases much too convenient (by the way, going forward, I want you to start equating the word 'convenient' with 'easy spending') but there are ways in which we can regain control.

My top tip is to **delete all your saved card payments from websites** – PayPal, Google Pay, Amazon, the lot. If it is easy to pay, chances are you will. Using the internet to shop is already too easy – you don't even have to leave your bed to do it! You can access it anywhere you go, meaning you can also spend money anywhere you go. But if you physically have to go and get your payment card or details every time you want to purchase something, you might realise that you don't really need the thing at all. You're giving yourself an opportunity to rethink your impulse purchase.

In the same way, you should **unlink your bank details from your phone's digital wallet**. We can pay for almost anything now with a just a quick tap of our phone, and that too is much too easy. You have a bank card, so go back to basics and just use that. Or, even better, use cash. Using cash for any purchases makes those spends real in a way that a card cannot. There is something psychological about seeing physical cash and handing it over. You have physical proof of your actions when you deal in coins and notes. Holding the money you have had to work for is powerful because it increases your sense of its value. It is a tangible reminder that, however you work or earn money, you are trading your time for cash.

You will also want to do all you can to avoid temptation. We've already looked at ways to identify your triggers and to use that self-knowledge to recognise the people, places and emotions that lead to spending, but there are some actionable tips to help you stay strong.

First, **unsubscribe from newsletters and offers that encourage you to spend money.** An email is a direct line from company to customer and so can be more than forty times more effective at getting you to shop than Facebook and Twitter. You signed up to the email list because you were interested in a particular business, so you were already engaged, so it is easy for the company to strike with offers and discounts galore. An email feels personal in a way that an online ad does not – that discount is for you, and only you. Sure, let's just click that link and see what this is. Of course you'll like it, didn't you sign up for the email list? If you want to save money, you need to have all temptations out of sight and mind.

Next, you should **unfollow anyone on social media that encourages you to spend but brings no real value to your life.** I have a following on Instagram, and I am obsessed with budgeting. So many people watch my Instagram stories, and we all somehow feel connected. Occasionally I will do Instagram ads with products that I love or that I think might be beneficial to my audience. My audience knows me, and I am sure they trust me, so they take my recommendations seriously. Brands will want to capitalise on that rapport – that is why many content creators are called influencers. I see nothing wrong with this personally – ads are a necessary means for the creator to earn enough money to continue to create the content you like. However, if you're following someone, you are already in awe of that person's lifestyle, and if all you see is the hit-this-link tab, it can be very tempting to want to buy into that stylised narrative. If a constant sales pitch is all they can bring to the table, then you need to pull the plug.

Next, you need to **stop browsing social media before bed**. This is good practice for all sorts of reasons – quality of sleep being top of the list – but the closer we get to bedtime, the more tired we are, and the more susceptible to targeted ads we become. We buy for so many reasons, and our tendency to impulse-buy is often heightened by a lack of sleep. It has even been documented that those shops target the vulnerable with late-night offers. I had an experience with this after I had my first child. During the day I was busy with a newborn baby – she was my sole focus, and all my attention was for with little time for me. I became a stranger to myself. I lost touch with who I was and would compare myself to celebrity mothers and all the other new mammies I saw on the internet. I felt worse about my appearance every time I looked. As if by fate, late one night (or I should say, early one morning), an ad popped up from a famous online shop. I decided there and then I would get a whole new wardrobe. I spent €400 in one night getting entirely new outfits in a size smaller than I was. I felt so chuffed and proud of myself. The following day, I woke up and did not remember anything. Then I received an email to say that my order was on its way. I did not cancel it, nor did I go down to a size 10. That was money I wasted on a decision made because I thought spending money would solve my self-image issues. Needless to say, it did not.

So, put down those phones at night, especially if you feel financially unwell whilst reading this book.

Finally, and this is a more general point, you need to be **mindful of what your money is worth**. You may think nothing of grabbing a sneaky takeaway – 'Aw, Santis, sure it's only €20!' – but do not ever speak casually about your money. It is never 'only' anything. Even if you are working in a job you love, you have had to sell your time in exchange for that money; and if you are in a job you hate – as many people are – just think of how many hours extra you will have to work to pay for every single thing you want to buy. That in itself should get you motivated to make changes.

You *can* keep your spending under control, you just need to keep reminding yourself that your time is precious, and that your money has a better place to go today.

Create a money calendar

You should by now have a list in front of you of all the spends you need to make (your needs), and all the ones you are willing to make (your wants). But what do you do with all that information?

My advice is to use a **MONEY CALENDAR** – a document that works like a regular calendar, but you use it to keep track of payment and income dates and amounts. You can use your phone or computer for this, but I feel that it is more impactful to use a physical product. Seeing is believing, and there is nothing like having a visual reminder of where your money is going laid out clear as day in front of you. It helps you identify at a glance when all bills are due to go out from your account, and when the money is coming in – particularly helpful if you work freelance or get paid different income streams – helping you stay organised and in control.

To get the most from your money calendar:

- Include the dates you expect each and every stream of income to come into your account.
- Include the dates each expense will go out of your account – include within that your mortgage/rent, direct debit payments, all bills and so on.
- Colour-code all entries. Get some good old-fashioned highlighters, categorise the type of payment/income, and give each category their own colour. You can even choose separate colours to indicate from which account each expense payment is coming.
- Set reminders in your phone a day before each transaction.
- Make a note of your saving goals for that month (an essential step, as it will be a constant reminder of your *why*).
- Include any No Spend Days you have planned (more on these in Chapter 8).
- Take a photo and set it as your new screensaver.
- Review your money calendar every time you get paid.

MAY MONEY CALENDAR 2022

SUNDAY	MONDAY	TUESDAY	WEDNESDAY
1 Property management €30 **Children allowance €280**	2 Drop-in dance classes €15	3 **Wages €3000**	4 Loan repayments €380
8 Property management €30	9 Drop-in dance classes €15	10 Phone bill €12.99	11 Fitness app €10
15 Property management €30	16 Drop-in dance classes €15 Netflix €20.99	17 Swimming €180 Loan €55	18 Car insurance €90 Gym €21
22 Property management €30	23 Drop-in dance classes €15	24 Electricity €174,50	25 Mortgage €1500
29 Property management €30	30 Drop-in dance classes €15	31 Coffee €10	

THURSDAY	FRIDAY	SATURDAY
5 Broadband €55 Petrol €65	6 Food shop €80 Takeaway €65	7 Family fun day €100
12 Spotify €12 Petrol €65	13 Food shop €80	14 Communion €50
19 Gymnastics €90 Petrol €65	20 Food shop €80 Takeaway €20	21 Dinner €60
26 Petrol €65 Crêche fees €382	27 Food shop €80	28 Communion €50

TOTAL INCOME 3,280.00
TOTAL EXPENDITURE 4,098.87
DEFICIT -818.48

The clarity a money calendar can offer will enable you to plan your finances more effectively, aiding you in ensuring the money you need at any given time will be in your account (meaning no cheeky direct debit bounce-back charges). You'll know what bills and costs are coming up so you can plan, manoeuvre and prepare your money to be in the right place at the right time.

Preparing your calendar and writing out each demand on your money also provides you with another opportunity to reflect on your wants and needs and analyse what is serving you, what you are getting value for money from and what figures you don't like the look of. Then make the effort to cut any dead weight you feel still remains! I call this 'the tremendous thinning' because I love a sparse money calendar. Not only is it a sexy look – it means that everything I have on there is because of a conscious decision.

This can be a pivotal tool in your financial journey and is one that I would advise you not to overlook.

Mentor's Notes
- Your *why* will be the driving force to keep you going when things get tough.
- Take the time to identify all your transactions.
- Do a digital clean-up and cut anything from your spending that is no longer serving you.

CHAPTER 3:

BUDGETS

So now that you have a better idea of the condition your finances are in, it's time to look at getting yourself **FINANCIALLY ORGANISED**. You must tell your money where to go rather than wondering where it went, and to do that, you need to set a **BUDGET.** A lot of us are not transparent with ourselves about our money so it is mindboggling to understand the possibilities that seeing your finances laid out in front of you can bring you.

The importance of budgeting

A budget, like money itself, is simply a tool. It is a map and a guide for your money that will aid you as you unlearn behaviours obtained during early environmental development (we don't just rectify bad money habits overnight; we are in the business of constantly unlearning and creating better behaviours around money). But more than that, having a budget will reduce your stresses around finance.

The best way to understand the importance of budgeting

is to think of your household as a business. Every business starts with a dream. A person will have an idea, then generate a business plan to see what is viable and what is not. Bigger companies will come with a finance department, but even small companies, sole traders and freelancers must be mindful of their budget – they need to have a plan that helps create focus and keep the business in line with its financial targets.

We need to apply this thinking to our household budget. Instead of a business plan, we should prepare our personal financial plan, filled with the most daring dreams for our life. Many people don't. Instead, as I mentioned before, they firefight. They are not proactive with their finances, and instead just deal with things when the time comes. But this is not enough! We need to know what is going on within our homes and lives, and a budget is a simple tool that will give you that level of awareness.

Done well, a budget will:

- empower you and help you reclaim control of your finances;
- offer the clarity you need to know where your finances are at any given time;
- change your outlook towards money;
- align your spending and saving habits to help you reach your financial goal. It takes the figures out of your head and makes what was a dream an achievable reality;

- encourage you to spend money in a conscious way, meaning no guilt or shame;
- enable you to acquire the essential things.

Remember, a budget doesn't limit you, it makes you fly – it helps you make short-term changes that can bring you long-term gain.

Why people avoid budgeting

I've met a lot of people who realise with total bewilderment that they do not have basic budgeting skills. But really, the odds are stacked against us from the very beginning as there is a severe lack of education about personal finance in our schools.

I would love to see proper budgeting become a part of every school's curriculum. I have spoken to some teachers about it, and their view is that personal finance is a subject that may be best for parents to teach, because money is such a personal thing.

I do understand their point, but I also think this is contra-dictory in many ways – our personal finances are indeed a very personal thing, but at the moment many of our children are being taught about money by financial institutions such as credit unions, businesses who will only act in their own self-interest in the long run. Education around personal finance should first and foremost look after the individual, not the institutions. Any institution that offers you a loan has, as their primary purpose, profit and loss. Although the credit union is members-based, and a more positive institution in many ways than banks, I do wonder – should they be the one teaching our children about savings, instead of the state? Their aim is not only to educate our children, but to attract more customers, and they target those customers in their formative years. There is a level of trust involved here, because if the school trusts their local credit union to educate children on finances, and I trust the school to teach my children, then that gives the impression that by extension I also trust the credit union to educate my children. Those children grow up to become the parents, who relay to their children the only financial education they've known – that of the financial institutions – and the cycle goes on. Yes as a parent we should be educating our children about money at home too, but if the parent has also come out of this same financial education, then I'm not sure it's possible for them to have the necessary tools to help educate their children in a new way.

I joined the credit union in school to save, yet a few years later everyone in my circle was getting a loan and so I did too. For years, I saw the credit union as my salvation. I kept hearing how much they do for the community and how they sponsor local sports teams. I love that, but there is a discord – when I visit my local credit unions there is never any mention of saving, but you can see loans on offer for every occasion. It all comes from our lack of education around money.

And it's no wonder that people shy away from budgeting if they have no experience of it. But what did surprise me, when I did a questionnaire asking people what they thought about budgeting, were the incredibly negative words that came to people's minds: cheap, tightwad, cringe, scabby, planner, controlling, no fun, boring, prison, calculating. Yes, there were some positive terms in there too – freeing, focus, debt-free, freedom – but the truth is, budgeting mostly has a (very undeserved) bad rap. There is always a reason that we avoid the things that can benefit us, the things we know we need to do, so I'm here to push back against some of the common excuses that surround budgeting.

> **The scarcity excuse:** *'If I start budgeting, I would not be able to get everything I want.'*

Depending on our view of money – remember those money personality types! – budgeting can tap into our scarcity mindset; or one of *lack* (where we look at how much money we *need* rather than how much we have). This is where we look at things through a lens of deprivation.

> **Counter:** Although it takes time to adjust our mindsets, a budget will separate our *wants* from our *needs*. We do not need another T-shirt because our favourite influencers tell us, 'You just gotta have it!' Having a budget will give you the confidence to say, 'No, actually I don't.'

If I am honest, before I started on my debt-clearing journey there was a deep-rooted shame in knowing that all I had to do was stop spending, but it was so difficult for me to let go. I didn't want to be left out of anything. I wanted to have money for things – it didn't matter whether they were nice or not. It was only when I started budgeting that I learned I had been so obsessed with acquiring more that I had stopped appreciating what I already had . . . and I had so much to be grateful for.

> **The Fear excuse:** *'If I start budgeting, I wouldn't be able to keep up with my friends; I would be moving in a different way from them. It would make me stand out.'*

Fear can be a great motivator, and yes, it was advantageous for our ancestors to have that fear for survival. However, now most of us are afraid of the unknown and uncomfortable with change, even when we know it might be good for us. And look, it is our brain's job to protect us so if budgeting is new and it's something our brain is unaccustomed to dealing with, it will give you every excuse to avoid, avoid, avoid. It will naturally feel that leaving our comfort zone is risky.

> **Counter:** Why are we so worried about what others think? Why is it so important to please others? I would even be so bold as to say that when you please others first, you cannot satisfy yourself. We need to put ourselves first; we need to be able to sleep without thinking about where we owe money, and we need

to be able to have *proper* connections with our friends without being panicked by the thought of how much the coffee we've just ordered is costing us.

When I stopped and realised how my energy was constantly changing depending on the people around me, it was an eye-opener. I'd been afraid to say no to people because I thought I might lose years of friendships. I started thinking about who my high-value friends are (those who want you to be you and nothing more, because you are enough). This was a harsh realisation. If I wanted to protect my financial well-being, I needed to manage the energy entering my life.

I had to do a lot of painful weeding. It felt as though I was being cheap at first, but I realised that if saying no to something I cannot afford offends you, then I feel insulted when you are in my presence. It was so empowering, and yes, I was afraid, but the numbers were not lying, and I was finally getting my eight hours of restful sleep!

The Difficulty excuse: *'Budgeting is too complicated – I'll never figure out how to do it.'*

When some people think of budgeting, the word 'difficult' is the first that comes to mind, or they think that you must be good at maths.

Counter: Budgeting is a habit, and like all great habits you may find it difficult at the start. You just need to shift your mindset. To create great sleeping habits, you need to have a great bedtime routine; to be more proactive, you need to plan; to be the best version of yourself, you need to practise; and to budget, you need to do the same – you just need to make it part of your everyday life. Do it often enough, and you'll do it without thinking.

I'm not going to sugar-coat it – budgeting can be tricky to get the hang of at the start. You are about to go into the unknown, do a deep-dive into your finances. Some days the numbers may not add up; sometimes you may think, 'I don't want to do this today.' You might even consider quitting altogether. But it is on these days that you need to remind yourself of your *why*. It is essential that you keep going.

Budgeting is not something from which you get a rush of adrenaline or instant gratification. **DELAYED GRATIFICATION** is what you are looking for. All your little changes will soon add up, and what that does for your personal growth is life-altering. You are creating a lifestyle that will sustain your mental well-being.

As a spender, I realised I depended a lot on instant gratification. I became addicted to the thrill of spending. When I spent money, my brain released endorphins and dopamine, and what started as a reward for me became purely about the addiction to that dopamine release. It became a way to hide from myself. Once I realised this, I had to create areas within my budget where I could somehow build in opportunities for that instant gratification. So I would set myself little milestones, and reward myself when I reached them. For example, once I'd had ten No Spend Days (more on those in Chapter 8) I allowed myself to buy a coffee from my favourite barista. It felt good, it felt earned and it was satisfying.

The 'not earning enough' excuse: 'I don't have enough money left at the end of the week in order to budget.'

Many people look at their bank account at the end of the week and see no money, so they think they already have an idea of how their finances are going. They feel that there is only a need to budget when you make a certain amount of money.

Counter: If you cannot manage your money when you earn less, you cannot manage your money when you earn more.

The fact that you may find yourself in deficit at the end of every payday is a great reason to start telling your money where to go instead of wondering where it went. When I realised that, it was as if a light bulb had come on in my head. Suddenly I was conscious of all the tiny spends that were leading me straight into the red.

My friend Olivia was always sound with her money, and she would look at me appalled as I went on about loan after loan. She always liked nice things, but luckily, her grandmother and mother were savvy budgeters, and she listened to them. So she saved hard for her clothes and bags and looked after them. She didn't buy clothes every week but invested in quality pieces. She was sensible; I was not. If I'm honest, I thought her spending habits were boring, so I stopped discussing money with her. Even when her mam tried to explain her budgeting method to me, I was a long way from being ready to listen. I just put it down to them having more money than me, and not that they were more mindful of the money they did have.

The stay oblivious excuse: *'What I don't know won't hurt me.'*

In some ways it can be easier to just try and ignore that you are constantly reaching for the credit card, even though you have already taken out loans left, right and centre. It can be heartbreaking to sit down and face how bad things may have become.

Counter: Facing the truth is usually the most challenging part of being financially unwell. The reality is, you are making a conscious decision to avoid dealing with your money, and that reality will raise its ugly head whether we want it to or not.

The thing is, hiding from your finances is easier said than done. I did everything in my power not to look at my loans or my finances. I worked harder, got more credit, and even hired another childminder so I could work more hours, yet I could not understand why I could hardly breathe. I was in such a dark place. Why was I always playing catch-up? I had a pain in my chest every time payday arrived, or when I'd walk past the post box and spot an envelope with another bill in it.

Then one day, all that changed. I sat down and listed everything I owed, and it was a weight off my mind, which had been operating entirely in survival mode for too long. I looked at the piece of paper and, honestly, I owed €10,000 less than I thought I owed.

And even better, now I had given myself a starting point.

The uncooperative partner excuse: 'My partner will not be on board with this.'

There are many reasons why people may feel anxious about having frank conversations with their partners about money: perhaps one or the other has hidden debts; maybe the partner is the one to manage the household accounts; maybe the couple keeps their finances separate; and maybe money talk causes so many arguments that people want to avoid it altogether.

Counter: Talking to our loved ones about money is more important than ever. The trick is to sit down and be honest in a non-accusatory fashion. Make budgeting a part of your grander purpose together. Be prepared to have a unique way of looking at money and work together to compromise. When something goes wrong, full transparency and a non-blaming scenario is the name of the game.

It is essential to understand each other's relationship with money (that's where our money personalities come in). If you can understand how your partner views money, then you can work on finding common ground, a path on which you can you move forward together. Everyone needs to feel comfortable sharing. A relationship is a partnership, and both parties need to work towards a common goal with mutual agreement. It is also a wonderful way of setting boundaries. And when you reach those little victory milestones, why not reward yourself as a couple?

I am currently a single parent. I have spent a lot of time thinking about my past relationships, and even though I did not think at the time that money played a direct role in ending those relationships, upon reflection, it did! In one relationship, the weight of managing the money was placed on me. In another, we kept our finances separate. I do not see anything wrong with having separate accounts, but a couple needs to prioritise their bills, outgoings and savings together. I walked away from both resentful and mistrustful, and I realise now that how I handled money within each relationship has affected my feelings towards them. I genuinely believe that a relationship has to be a partnership with some shared goals, and finances need to be something for which a couple share common ground. Money plays too big a role to just ignore. I want to know your likes and dislikes, but also in time I want to know your credit score and your financial plan.

So before you make up another excuse not to budget, just know that it is okay to put your hands up and say, 'I messed up.' You need to realise that many of us have messed things up. The important thing is that we learn from our mistakes and try to get ourselves back on track.

My mission is to get you to look at budgeting from a place of love.

Different budgeting methods

When you break it down, *a budget is simply your income minus your expenses, then the remainder goes towards whatever goals you might be trying to achieve.* You create a plan for your money, spend less than you earn and invest the rest towards your financial goals. Whether you are clearing debt or saving your emergency fund, a budget can help.

A budget should be done yearly, as an overview, and then just before every pay cycle. It should be consistent and habitual.

For the best part of 2019, I was a humble student of the Japanese Kakeibo method – so named as it uses a *kakeibo* (a book/ledger of accounts) for tracking purchases. It was invented in 1904 by Hani Motoko, the first female journalist in Japan – can we get an amen? – and has at its core an emphasis on mindful spending and saving. It forces you to take a careful look at your spending rather than spending mindlessly and then regretting it. It promotes an essential change in mindset.

The Japanese believe that financial stability is essential for healthy well-being and that tidy finances are as powerful as having a clean house. The philosophy of Kakeibo represents a pathway to balance and calm . . . with all things in life, we must have balance.

Thanks to following this plan and developing my own methods (Kakeibo was really influential when I designed and produced my own ledger, *The Budget Mindset Planner*), I realised that simple is always better.

There are many variations and types of budgeting approaches out there, designed to suit all types of money personalities, so there is bound to be one that resonates with you. Here are some of them:

- Zero-Based Budgeting
- Priority-Based Budgeting
- The Cash-Envelope System
- Pay Yourself First
- 50-30-20
- Kakeibo
- The Four Families Budgeting Method

Zero-Based Budgeting

This method is for someone super-focused on their goals and their habits around money. Many budgets take the previous budget into consideration, so it can be easy to get into a rut: things become repetitive, and every month is a copy of the last. A Zero-Based Budget does not do that: it forces you to commit to habit-building straight away.

Under this approach, *every cent has a name and a job to do*. However, every time you sit down and budget, you need to justify the importance of each spend. You earn money, assign it to a spending category and move on with your life until the next payday. When you give every cent a purpose, it creates clarity around what you value. It forces you to question the relevance of your goals and your spending habits every time you put pen to paper or input your budget digitally. It can be challenging because people find it hard to justify allocating all their money to the different expenses. Budgeting like this can impact on your behaviour towards your goals.

For a Zero-Based Budget:
- You need to have a clear goal that you want to achieve within each pay period and an overall goal for yourself: a yearly target.
- Make a list of your income and expenses. All of these should be accounted for. This is important, and although I am not too fond of the word 'ruthless', I use it for impact here: you need to be ruthless when sieving out this information.
- You need to allocate all your expenses to distinct categories. Some examples are mortgage, food shop, petrol. Once you allocate that money, there is no turning back.

- Every month is a learning experience for the simple reason that every month starts with a clean slate.
- Zero-based means that there should not be *any* money left at the end of the budgeting process.

Case Study

Michelle is a single woman who dreams of owning her own house. She earns €1,750 per month and makes sure every cent of that salary is given a specific purpose.

Outgoing	Cost	Total remaining from salary (€1,750)
Food	€240	€1,510
Rent	€710	€800
Amenities (broadband, heating and electricity, etc.)	€250	€550
Direct debits (health insurance, rates, etc.)	€100	€450
Travel (bus fare)	€50	€400
Socialising	€150	€250
Debt repayment	€100	€150
House deposit fund	€150	€0.00

At this rate, by the end of the year she will have saved €1,800 into her house deposit fund.

Pros	Cons
It is cost-effective, because you must constantly adjust it.	It can be daunting at the start to try and analyse every category and question where every cent is going.
Instead of adding different spending categories, you prioritise the most important ones in your life.	It can be time-consuming, at least initially, to get into the groove of things.
It is motivating – it asks you where your money needs to go every payday, right now.	You will get it wrong before you get it right.
It enables you to focus on what is essential in your life.	~~~~~~~~

Priority-Based Budgeting

Priority-Based Budgeting is a brilliant method to use to change your mindset around money. Your expenses are based on your priorities: your starting income is divvied out by funding the things that matter to you first. *It is a way to align your money to your needs, goals and values about money.* It limits emotional and last-minute buys and is excellent for low-income earners, those with significant expenses and beginner budgeters living payday to payday.

For a Priority-Based Budget:
- Create a list with all your outgoings, and then reorganise this list in order of importance. This list is the most revisited part of this budget and your goals.
- Start with the most important thing on the list and allocate to it the money it will need. This should be

your basic needs – food, housing, utilities, transport and childcare – and they should be prioritised over everything.
- Then move on to the next thing on the list, and so on, and so on.
- Have a hard look at how much you can minimise your outgoings by figuring out the minimum you need to survive.
- Put the extra towards your goals, whatever they are.

Remember, things pop up, and always seem to do so just as you get in the groove, so please make sure you adjust your budget in order of priority. So, say you started to budget this week but your fridge breaks – getting a new fridge goes almost to the top of the list. The things that you have at the bottom of your priority lists, such as movie nights or a new dress, can act in some way as a cushion, or as a temporary emergency fund (at least until you have one in place, because setting up an emergency fund is a priority – see Chapter 4).

Case Study
Ciara's monthly salary is €1,660. She wants to establish an emergency fund and pay off her credit card debt, and she knows that there is room in her outgoings to make some cuts, so she decides to prioritise her expenses.

Santis O'Garro

Before prioritising	
Outgoing	**Cost**
Rent	€450
Socialising	€300
Food	€200
Utilities	€150
Takeaway lunches	€100
Beauty and fashion	€100
Bus fare	€80
Health insurance	€80
Work Christmas fund	€80
Credit card minimum repayment	€40
Credit Union	€40
Gym membership	€40
Total	€ 1,660

After prioritising	
Outgoing	**Cost**
Rent	€450
Food (including homemade lunches)	€100
Utilities	€250
Health insurance	€80
Bus fare	€40
Credit card minimum repayment	€40
Socialising (reduced)	€100
Beauty and Fashion	€100
Work Christmas fund	€80
Takeaway lunches	€0
Credit Union	€0
Gym membership	€0
	€1,240

When Ciara reordered her outgoings in order of priority, it became apparent where the cuts had to be made. She realised she was spending nearly the same amount of money socialising as she was on her dwelling. She also decided to cancel her gym membership in favour of walking to work two or three times per week, thus also saving on bus fare.

By prioritising her outgoings, she now has €370 left every month, which she puts towards her emergency fund and debt repayment.

Pros	Cons
It takes the worrying out of budgeting.	It can be overwhelming to start.
It helps to align your values with your money.	It's time-consuming in the beginning.
It removes stress around money.	It can be hard to give up certain things.
It keeps you organised and planning ahead.	It can make you reluctant to spend on your wants at all.

The Cash-Envelope System

When we budget using digital methods, it can sometimes be hard to stay the course as the money we *do* spend might not feel like money – it can be hard to follow through. You might have set aside €400 in your bank account for Christmas, but one day something catches your eye, and suddenly the Christmas money has been spent on a new set of curtains.

The Cash-Envelope System makes you accountable. With

this method, if say you are saving €400 for Christmas, you withdraw €400 from the bank and put it in a 'Christmas' Cash Envelope; then anything you purchase using cash from that envelope can only be Christmas-related. *It encourages you to stay loyal to your budget because you cannot spend what you do not have.*

People tend to complicate the Cash-Envelope System method, but as much as it limits your impulse-buying and changes your mindset around money, it is not complex. It is an effective, practical and fun (if a little old-fashioned) way of beginning your budgeting journey, and it involves taking your budget back to basics. It puts manners on your money.

For the cash envelope system:
- You will need a sheet of paper/notebook, a pen and some envelopes. Your sheet is where you track your expenses when using your cash envelope.
- Write out the following headings on your page: *Date | Description | Amount | +/- Balance*
- Each envelope will represent a certain category of spending (e.g. food, birthday gifts, socialising, etc.), and into each envelope you should place, in cash, the amount of money you can allocate to that category. You can either write the relevant spending category on each envelope, or on a separate sheet of paper for continuity. I prefer the latter as it is nice to have an ongoing record in which you can reflect on your growth. It also saves on wasting envelopes.

- As you add to your cash envelope or take money out, you should, on your tracker sheet, make note of the date, the transaction, whether you're adding or subtracting (use + or – beside the transaction amount) and the balance. This should always match what cash you currently have in the envelope.

So, if your weekly food budget is €60 then, when you get paid, you withdraw €60 in cash and place it in an envelope. That is the money you have to spend on food until the next day you budget.

Date	Description	Amount +/−	Balance
26 June	Weekly shop	−€45.00	€15
30 June	Top-up shop	−€10.00	€5

The monthly tracker is also ideal if you are trying to save within a limited time or have a significant expense. For this, you can apply the **SPLIT METHOD**. Say you want to save for a holiday, for example, a girls' trip that will cost €1,000, but you only have five months to save. You'll know straight away that you'll need to put €200 per month in your envelope to get there.

Cash-Envelope Tracker

Another way of tracking your cash envelope is to:

- Create an cash envelope for each category.
- List out the twelve months horizontally on the envelope;
- Write under each month and create two boxes;
- One box is for the projected amount you would like to save towards the category;
- The second box is what you saved in the envelope each month.

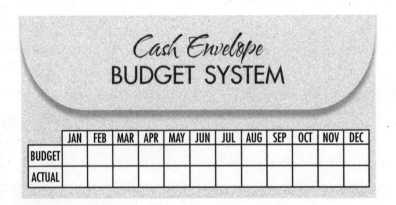

The Cash Envelope System does not need to be complicated: you just use envelopes as a more hands-on way to portion out your money, so it can work in tandem with other budgeting methods (it works perfectly alongside a zero-based budget).

It can even be fun! There is a whole online movement dedicated to this method and, while you can use plain old envelopes you have lying around the house as you get accustomed to using them, there are plenty of pretty envelope designs and free templates out there (including on my website). There is also an undeniable sense of achievement in watching that cash pile up!

Case Study

David works in a stressful job. He has recently had a breakdown in his marriage and now finds himself anxious all the time. His only outlet has been spending money. As he scrolled through social media, he would see his peers with their new gadgets, cars and perfect families. Without thinking, he would add some of the same products he'd seen his friends with to his trolley and before he could blink, he'd be at the checkout.

When David started his budgeting process, he noticed that these impulse/emotional spending habits were causing significant strain on his bank account. He was advised to transfer a few expenses he would subconsciously spend on his card. David decided to pay most of his expenses in the form of cash. Some things like his electricity were unavoidable and he didn't want to miss his direct-debit discount. By paying with cash, he became aware of his spending habits as he could physically see the money he was spending, instead of reaching for his card at different moments to impulsively buy things. But because he had unlinked his bank from all his shopping accounts and he did a zero-based budget it was impossible to keep up his impulse-spending habit. There was no money lying around his account that wasn't accounted for in his budgeting. In the supermarkets he was more cautious with his money as he knew that what was in his envelope was all he had.

After doing this for one pay cycle, he noticed a decrease

in his spending almost immediately. He had money in his envelope to carry forward to next month. This gave him a sense of satisfaction and he felt rewarded for his good work. Because David put aside his monthly self-care amount, he was able to spend on himself guilt-free and more intentionally. Every month, he would be filled with pride as his budgeting meant he had both excess money to save and he could also now buy the things he wanted, while still operating within his budget.

Pros

Limits spending as it makes you conscious of where your money is going.

Helps you control your spending. You cannot spend what you do not have.

The physical representation of your money creates more internal value.

Reduces emotional spending.

It is highly satisfying to watch your money build up.

Means less stress because you know you have accounted for this expense.

Builds a positive relationship of respect for your money.

Cons

It can be time-consuming always going back to the bank.

You must physically go to the cash machine.

Requires trial and effort to get it right.

People do not like using cash for hygiene reasons.

People do not like keeping large sums of cash at home.

It could seem too limited at the start.

It might not help you to get bargains online.

~~~~~~~~~~

Pay Yourself First

Pay Yourself First is a method recommended by most financial advisors. It is sometimes called a reverse budget and can be something to work towards. It involves putting money in savings and investment accounts before looking at paying bills. It is an excellent way of pushing towards a goal, as it prioritises savings over all else – before you even see the money for the rest of your expenses, you have already prioritised your future transactions. It forces a person to keep their expenses to a minimum to facilitate this.

I agree with it in principle, but I do feel that it is only suitable for people at a particular stage of their budgeting journey: those who are goal-focused, earn a decent wage and dislike being disorganised with their budget; or those who have been budgeting for quite a while, know what they earn and their pay-out is like clockwork. If you like a challenge and are engaged in a lifestyle overhaul, then this method is for you.

So, say you want to get a new car. Under this method, before you do anything else, you would make sure that you allocated the amount you wish to put away for the car, and then live off the rest.

You should only really attempt this method once you have a very detailed and specific idea of your outgoings (by giving yourself a money NCT) and you understand the importance of regular budgeting and of getting to know your figures. It would be worth your while to read books on money management and invest in your financial education by consistently learning what other tips and tricks are out there to give you more freedom with your income.

For a Pay-Yourself-First budget:
- Calculate what percentage of your income you want to pay yourself first (the best way to make this payment is by automating your transactions).
- Then split the remaining funds among your other categories.

This is undoubtedly a hard method to get to grips with. It is scary to even contemplate not paying your bills first, especially if you are struggling to manage, payday to payday. But this is a good method to aspire to. Just start small, look at your budget and ask yourself, 'What I am willing to put towards my future when I get paid?' Then, as your journey continues, that figure can grow.

My view is that, although it can seem daunting, the best way to approach this one is to do it in your own time and according to your own values. I believe in sacrifice, but it is essential to plan and do things when the timing feels right for you. Your priority might be to focus on getting your debt cleared before concentrating on anything else.

It took me two years to get to the point of paying myself first, and you know what, even with the attractiveness of compound interest, I was not mentally ready *then* to start thinking the way I think now, and **that is okay**. Just know that this method is something to work towards. There's no point having all the money in the world if you cannot enjoy it.

Case Study

Julie wants to buy a house.

Her Income is €5000 per month

Her expenses are €4000 per month

Julie automates a monthly payment of €1000 per month towards her house deposit before she looks at any other expense in her budget.

Although Julie earns a decent wage, she is frustrated by the lack of progress. It just felt like she was adding money to her house deposit as a part of a checklist rather than making her deposit her top priority.

When she pays herself first, she ensures that the surplus money she would have had is now going straight to her main priority (her house deposit), which builds faster and maintains her motivation to keep saving.

Pros	Cons
You prepare yourself for your future straightaway.	It can be hard to stay disciplined.
Can lead to a significant mindset shift.	It could leave you struggling elsewhere in life.
Encourages you to focus on levelling up.	It does not always work for every situation, and a change of circumstances can mentally mess up your goals and dreams.
Keeps focus on cost-cutting.	
Encourages cost control.	
Helps you gain confidence.	
With saving, you are benefitting from compound interest.	

50-30-20

This percentage-based budgeting method was created by mother-and-daughter team, Elizabeth Warren and Amelia Warren Tyagi, and is an effortless way to manage your expenses confidently. Without involving too much thinking, all you need to do is divide your after-tax income into three pots – 50 per cent, 30 per cent and 20 per cent – and assign each pot to a spending category.

For a 50-20-30 budget:
- 50 per cent of your after-tax income will go towards your basic needs; things that are essential to your survival – food, housing, utilities, transport and childcare (I'll go into these a little more in the Four Families method).
- 30 per cent is allocated to your wants; the little luxuries and non-essential items that you have in your budget because they make life comfortable, things like eating out, getting new clothes and your hobbies.
- 20 per cent goes to your savings, investments and debt repayment. Examples of this would be your emergency funds, pension, debts and investment portfolio.

It is so easy to get caught up and obsessed with funding our needs and wants, but this last category is just as important. We need to prioritise saving for an emergency – we should all be able to relax, knowing that that, financially, we would be okay if something happened.

This method offers a fantastic way to start your budgeting journey if you are unsure how to budget your money, especially if you do not have time to track your spending. I love the idea of balance with my money, and I love the simplicity of percentages, but I see them as a guideline. The exact 50-30-20 split may not always be possible (for example, if your mortgage is already half of your budget). It allows for an in-depth look at your money, and emphasises the need to track your spending to categorise it efficiently. It is a flexible and balanced method, giving you a template for the prioritisation of your needs, and shows that, with planning, you can have everything you need and want, plus be future-proof.

Case Study

Yvonne, a single parent on state benefits, earns €1,200 per month.

- 50 per cent of this will go towards her needs
  [€1,200 × 0.50 = €600]
- 30 per cent of this will go towards her wants
  [€1,200 × 0.30 = €360]
- 20 per cent of this will go towards her savings, debt repayment and emergency fund
  [€1,200 × 0.20 = €240]

Pros	Cons
Easy to calculate.	Might be intimidating for someone on a low income – it might put them off their budgeting journey.
An excellent outline to budget effectively.	
Easy to compartmentalise.	It may seem unrealistic to some.
It is achievable.	It requires a lot of discipline.
Makes it easy to automate your savings and debt repayments.	The exact 50-30-20 split may not always be possible.

The Four Families Method

This is a method that I came up with. It is possible to combine the different budgeting methods to make a budgeting plan that makes sense for you and your lifestyle. This method takes elements from Zero-Based budgeting, mixes them with some from Priority-Based budgeting and adds a dash of 50-30-20.

In it I have taken the different expenses we spend our money on and grouped them into four categories – or, as I like to call them, **FOUR FAMILIES**. I then arranged each family in order of priority, with the idea that, once you have paid for everything in the first family, you take any money you have left over and pass it on to the second family, and so on, and so on.

1)   THE WALL FAMILY

Within this category are all your basic, essential needs; things that you just cannot live without. I have also referred to these in the past as your foundations; the kind of things that, if you didn't have them, would keep you awake at night:

- **food** – and by this, I mean your weekly grocery shop not your takeaways as these are wants and belong in a different category.
- **utilities** – heat, water, electricity, gas.
- **housing** – rent/mortgage.
- **transport** – including your petrol or public transport. And, yes, depending on your situation, this can be an essential. If you cannot get to work, you cannot earn a wage.
- **childcare** – if you have children and don't have someone to look after them, you will not be able to work.
- **health insurance** – for many families, this is a necessity. Personally, health insurance is not something I would place here as it doesn't pertain to my family for different reasons, but this is another example of how what is defined as 'necessary' depends on your own circumstances.
- **clothing** – when I first started to budget, clothing was very much a need. But now, with swapping or buying preloved, we have an abundance of clothes. For me, the clothing expense belongs in a different family, but for others, it can be a necessity.

For most people using the Four Family Method, I suggest that they start here. If you're a low-income earner or only at the start of journey, the Wall Family is what you should take care of first. You'll be able to sleep at night and look at your family with pride, knowing that you're able to support them. You will know with confidence that you are able to meet your *needs*. You need to secure your Walls before you go another step further.

2) THE LONG FAMILY You've covered your basic needs, which means you are no longer firefighting. Now you can start to plan ahead for your wants – the expenses that come up time and again:

- meeting your minimum **debt repayment.**
- **broadband** – (unless you work from home, broadband is a want)
- **life insurance** – as a single mam in good health, I chose to prioritse life insurance for my children. It's an emotional decision but one that offers me peace of mind.
- **birthday fund**
- **back-to-school fund**
- **Christmas fund**

People nowadays tend to confuse their wants with their needs, but as you start to become more mindful about your spending, you start to realise how blurred our vision can get when it comes to the two. For example, food in general is a need but you do not *need* to buy crisps and jellies – they should go in your wants. As should the things in the Long Family: you do not need any of these things to live, but they improve your standard of living.

3) THE FUNDAYS FAMILY The first thing we do when we start to tighten our belts is cut out all the fun things. But everything needs balance, and if you can work your fun into your budget – even if it is something as simple as a coffee with a friend – then you can have it guilt-free. Under this category are the following:

- **TV streaming services/subscriptions**
- **other subscriptions** – for instance, Audible, Spotify, etc.
- **small treats** – a new lipstick, a trip to the cinema, hobby supplies.
- **your children's fun activities** – like swimming classes, gymnastics, or clubs.

The important thing here is that you take a careful conscious look at what will make you happy. Make sure the fun is worth the spend.

4) THE JONES FAMILY This last family is goal-based – it is directly connected to your *why*. What do you want from your budgeting journey? Instead of keeping up with the Joneses, you become the Joneses. This is where you start to fund your dream holiday; your dream home; your wedding; your emergency fund; extra debt repayments. Try your best to keep something for this family.

For a Four Families budget:
Wall Family
- Take your starting income and cover everything in

your Wall Family. If your funds do not stretch that far then you need to think about reviewing the amounts, you are spending on each. Try to keep your costs for these as low as possible.

- Whatever is left after covering the Wall Family becomes your new starting income. Pay for as much as you can from the Long Family ...
- ... then the Fundays Family ...
- ... then the Jones Family.

In this way, every cent of your income is accounted for, similar to the Zero-Based method.

Now, you should know by now that I believe that the most successful methods are those with a little flexibility, so if you are on top of your budget and you are budgeting week in and week out, then you may decide that you want start by paying yourself first. In that case, you can put the Jones Family first, instead of the Wall Family, and the Wall will come second. So if you want to say that every month no matter what, you will pay €140 into an investment fund, then that is the first thing you would do before you start splitting the pot between the Wall, the Long and the Fundays family categories.

Case Study

Ciara and her family didn't know where to start when choosing their budgeting method. They had money going out in all directions. They didn't know which was essential and what they could plan for in the future. Ciara's husband

Jack thought they needed a bit more fun, but Ciara wanted all their attention focused on their needs.

With the different families in this budget, Ciara and Jack could get what they needed from their household income.

The Wall Family was cared for so the family could have peace of mind.

The Long Family had money to keep up with debt repayments and to save funds for future events such as going back to school.

The Fundays were allocated money in the budget which meant that everyone could indulge in their hobbies guilt-free and have some family fun.

The Jones meant progress was being made towards their financial plan, like making extra debt payments and payments to their future goals.

Below are two examples of Four Families payday budget planners:

Method 1:

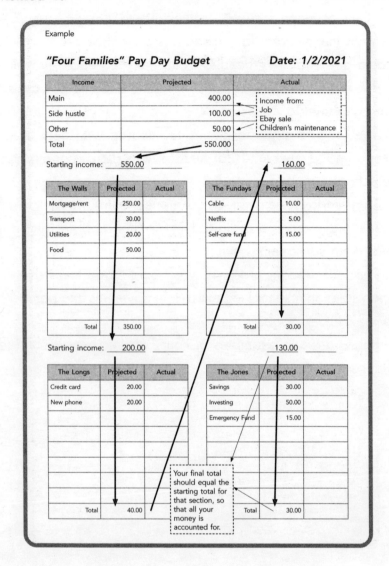

Example

"Four Families" Pay Day Budget   Date: 1/2/2021

Income	Projected	Actual
Main	400.00	Income from:
Side hustle	100.00	Job
Other	50.00	Ebay sale / Children's maintenance
Total	550.000	

Starting income: __550.00__   __160.00__

The Walls	Projected	Actual
Mortgage/rent	250.00	
Transport	30.00	
Utilities	20.00	
Food	50.00	
Total	350.00	

The Fundays	Projected	Actual
Cable	10.00	
Netflix	5.00	
Self-care fund	15.00	
Total	30.00	

Starting income: __200.00__   __130.00__

The Longs	Projected	Actual
Credit card	20.00	
New phone	20.00	
Total	40.00	

The Jones	Projected	Actual
Savings	30.00	
Investing	50.00	
Emergency Fund	15.00	
Total	30.00	

Your final total should equal the starting total for that section, so that all your money is accounted for.

Method 2:

"Four Families" Pay Day Budget   Date: 9/9/22.

Income	Projected	Actual
Main		
Side hustle		
Other		
Total		

Starting income: 500   480   6090   5590

The Walls	Projected	Actual
mortgage	175	175.00
Food	40	40.00
Electricity	25.00	25.00
Childcare	50.00	50.00
Insurance	9.10	9.10
Petrol	25.00	20.00
Property m.	15.00	1590
Total	339.10	334.10

The Fundays	Projected	Actual
Childrens Fun	10.00	10.00
Sewimming	10.00	10.00
Self Care	20.00	20.00
Karate	10.00	10.00
Netflix	–	–
Amazon	–	–
Dancing	5.00	5.00
Total	55.00	55.00

Starting income: 200.00   14590   590   90

The Longs	Projected	Actual
Childrens c	10.00	10.00
Life insurance	7.00	7.00
Gifts	20.00	20.00
Christmas	20.00	20.00
Phone	5.00	5.00
Broadband	8.00	8.00
Back 2 school	10.00	10.00
Car main	10.00	10.00
Total	100.00	90

The Jones	Projected	Actual
montserrat	590	90
Total	590	90

Bills   cash   10.00
110   185.00   SF

Pros	Cons
Easy to complete.	It can be tricky to start.
Perfect for a beginner budgeter.	Balancing is an ongoing process.
Allows you to understand your spending habits.	Somewhat time-consuming at the beginning.
Allows you to live without worry as your basics are taken care of.	Hard to categorise certain expenses.
Easy to maintain.	~~~~~~~~
Adaptable as your budget changes.	

Mentor's Notes

- There is a budgeting method out there for everyone.
- Shift your thinking and start to view your expenses in terms of priority.
- It is essential to know the difference between a want and a need.

CHAPTER 4:

DON'T PANIC! DEALING WITH DEBT

If your most pressing issue is debt – and I'm talking crippling, significant debt – then there are some things you can do to ease the pressure right now. I want you to forgive yourself for all your past money mistakes. Perfection is unattainable and we need to know that we have slip-ups but let's be accountable and keep it moving.

Prepare to clear your debt mindfully and with intention

Several debt repayment methods are available for those who want to tackle their debt. When I began my journey, and realised I needed to make a change for me and my family, I was €15,000 in debt. I told myself I was going to clear it in one year. I didn't know how or where to start. I knew that I didn't want to accumulate more debt, but I also didn't want to pay more interest than I had to with the debt I already had.

I have already pinpointed the importance of our environment in shaping our behaviours around money. Before I began my debt-free journey, I had created an environment around myself where debt was a means to an end. It was ordinary and almost necessary to sustain the standard of living to which I (and I'm sure many other people) had become accustomed to. It's important when you begin looking at your debt payoff, and how you're going to go about achieving it, to assess the situation with both your emotional and intellectual intelligence. In this section we'll look at some practical tips that you can apply to begin clearing your debt.

Make a commitment to not acquiring any more debt. I mean no more loans, no more spending on your credit cards. It's time to stop allowing debt to get in the way of your financial freedom.

LOOK AT YOUR STRESSORS. For me, my sources of stress were bills, especially bills that I was behind on; the constant phone calls and letters meant that I could only think of my life through a financial lens that was tinted red. Your stressors can be things like your

- credit union loans
- mortgage repayments
- bank charges for missed payments
- money owed to friends and family

To begin with, list everything you owe on a piece of paper. I mean *everything*. Include the amount, the interest rate, the date that the debt is due for repayment (if applicable) and anything else that might be relevant. Once your debts are listed out, you can easily assess them, and order them in importance by

- the highest interest
- the biggest monthly repayment
- what you owe to family and friends

From here, you can figure out a debt-free plan. First off, decide what order is best to tackle your debts. If family and friends are your priority and you feel they should be repaid first, then that's what you focus on. If you want to cut down on interest whilst tackling your debt, then focus on eradicating your high-interest debts first.

The next thing I would advise is to ring your lenders (including friends and family) and explain your situation to them: it might seem daunting, but it's always worth it. I was able to get a freeze on my mortgage repayment for three months. This gave me the breathing room to save money on my debt repayment and even get ahead on some payments. Headspace is something we lack when we have the burden of debt, and without knowing it you are mindlessly calculating your interactions and avoiding situations because of this. But facing it head-on by picking up the phone will let the lenders know exactly what is going on and in turn will let them inform you on what can be done to make life more liveable for you.

Clearing your debt means ideally not adding more to your existing debt, so it might seem obvious but it's important to stop adding non-essential spending to your credit cards. Freeze your cards or even cut them all up if you feel you need to.

One of your goals in this process should be to commit to bringing everything in your finances up to scratch. You don't want to have any outstanding payments. This gives you a level playing field and allows you to keep your house in order – there is no point focusing on one debt when you're unwittingly behind on something else with interest repayments adding up, costing you more money in the long term.

When I looked at my debt, I didn't have a lot of high-interest loans. My most significant loan was with my credit union, which also happened to be the loan I had with the highest interest. If you do have high levels of interest on debt however, such as on credit card debt, I'd recommend you use a **BALANCE TRANSFER CREDIT CARD**. Remember, not all debts – even some credit cards – are bad. Balance transfers are an incentive by credit card companies to attract new customers. I see these as a cheap loan. A very cheap loan. You are moving your balance to another account with a cheaper rate. It is very useful if you are on a high rate of interest. We know that some credit card interest rates can go incredibly high and if you can only afford paying a minimum on your end, this can end up compounding your repayments by paying interest on top of interest. It is important to be the master of this game, if you intend to play it.

Suppose you have a credit card with a balance of €1000 and an interest rate of 22.1 per cent, and you want to pay €35 per month; it would take you three years and five months to clear the balance with a total interest of €432.57. Or you can transfer the balance and pay for two years and five months. We would want to get that debt paid before the interest kicked in. So before you transfer anything, make sure you can clear the card within the interest-free period. So €1000 over the interest-free period of a year is €83.33 monthly with 0 per cent interest paid.

An Post currently offer a 0 per cent balance transfer for twelve months, while Avant Money offer 0 per cent for nine months. It's worth noting that this information on these rates was readily available on Switcher.ie or Bonkers.ie – two websites that are lifelines for comparing prices, budgeting and saving. If you're not disciplined enough to do this, stay away from this method. But if you are disciplined and have high-interest debts, it might be a great way to clear debt with minimum cost to yourself.

The Snowball Debt Repayment Method

I used this method in my own debt pay-off journey. It focuses on your smallest outstanding debt, which should be the quickest to clear. The idea is to throw any extra money each month towards that smallest debt whilst continuing to pay your minimum on your other debts. Finally, continue this process until you achieve a fast debt pay-off. I promise you this method is addictive. You would be on such a fast train. This momentum enabled me to pay off €15,027 of debt in twelve months. I achieved my goal by taking the following steps:

1. List out your debts.
2. Order them from lowest debt to the highest.
3. Make sure your debts payments are all up to date.
4. Proceed to pay the lowest debt first.
5. Continue to pay the minimum debt payment.
6. Every bit of money you save within your budget will go towards this smallest debt.
7. When the debt is paid you take the same energy and put that money towards the new lowest debt.
8. Like a snowball it will build as the debts roll into one.

I started paying €600 per month towards debt; by the time I finished it had snowballed to €1200.

Avalanche Debt Pay-Off

This method is great if you want to focus on paying back less interest and saving money in the long run. Something to remember is that while this method *will* save you money over time, it can be frustrating as it can be hard to create a sense of momentum.

The main idea with this method is to use any extra income, or savings made through your budget, to make increased repayments on the highest interest debt. As you do this, you continue paying back the minimum repayments needed on all your other debts. It is not the fastest debt repayment method, but it can be just as satisfying. When the debt with the highest interest is cleared, you roll over your increased repayment method to the next highest interest rate, and so it continues.

Emotional Debt Pay-Off

Money can be one of the main causes of family disputes, and a cause of real emotional stress. One of the reasons we don't like debt is that it feels like the lender is your master. The emotional debt pay-off method focuses on clearing debts owed to friends and family, to ease the emotional stress involved in those relationships. If you feel that owing money to your friends and family is stressful, why not remove that tension so you can figure out your next course of action for the rest of your finances? I think emotions play a huge part in our decision-making processes, and so once you can feel that the emotional strain is settled, you can tackle the rest of your debts using other methods – such as the debt snowball or debt avalanche method as normal.

It is hard to clear debt, especially emotionally, as you may have been using the debt to prop up a life you couldn't really afford. You invested in that life, and even though you knew something was off you kept investing in more to get the emotional release you needed and to live the lifestyle you thought you needed. Then, suddenly, you realise this was a bad investment, but you can't help but mourn the loss of a lifestyle you idealised and normalised. I know it took me a while to mourn my past life. It's very important, when clearing your debt, to let go of the lifestyle that the debt propped up, to allow yourself to say goodbye.

Mentor's Notes
- Debt is the biggest threat to financial freedom.
- Utilise the debt payment methods that best suit you and your situation to help clear your debts.
- Whether we like to admit it or not, debt can play havoc on your relationships if you owe money to friends and family, so just as with your financial institutions, it's best talk to your lenders.

CHAPTER 5:

EMERGENCY FUNDS AND SAVING FUNDS

After a certain amount of time budgeting, you will find that you get into the groove of things. This is when you need to start setting up your two significant funds: your **EMERGENCY FUND** (a pot of money that will cover you in case of emergency) and your **SAVING FUND** (a fund for planned future expenses).

It may be hard to differentiate between the two because for both, you are 'just saving'. But the difference is that one pot is preparing you for *just in case* and the other must cover actual expenses.

Let's take a look at the first of these, the emergency fund.

What is an emergency fund?

Also referred to as a rainy-day fund or get-out-of-jail fund, an emergency fund is simply a pot of money you should have set aside in case of emergencies. It is a safety net for when unexpected expenses arise. That is why I recommend that one of your first goals should be to set one up.

Most people start budgeting because they are financially unwell, and when you're in debt and broke, you are already worried. So when an unforeseen emergency spend pops up, it adds more stress to your already fragile financial well-being. It can feel as if the whole world is concocting tricks to break you with the many things that can go wrong. If you are living payday to payday, and you barely have enough money to fill your fridge, the last thing you need is for that fridge to break down.

An emergency fund can:

- **Prevent you sliding back into debt:** instead of reaching for your credit card in an emergency, you can take it from your emergency fund.
- **Build confidence:** it offers reassurance that, should anything happen outside of your control, you have money set aside to cover it.
- **Encourage budgeting:** just having an emergency fund is a significant win, but it also leaves you curious to see just how much further budgeting can take you.
- **Discourage unnecessary spending:** you will find ways to reduce your spending when you have an emergency fund because you know the work it took to save it.
- **Offer peace of mind:** a rainy day is unavoidable, but an emergency fund is your umbrella.
- **Increase awareness of your lifestyle cost:** you start looking at the liability attached to having more:

how much is this going to cost me? Could I keep up with the upkeep?

Your emergency fund should be accessible when you need it, but not too easy to get to if you are prone to withdrawing on impulse. I wouldn't be preoccupied with whether the account you choose is high interest or not, the important thing is that it is safe, and you can access it within a day. A post office or credit union account is ideal.

You might be thinking, 'But, Santis, isn't this just a savings account?' – well I'm here to tell you that although it is money that you have saved, it now has a different purpose. You want to always give your money a job and specific intention as, unless you classify what your savings are for, they have no real goal except to be there whenever you want or need them. And that kind of thinking can lead to you dip into the account whenever the notion takes you. Your emergency fund should not be accessed unless there is a genuine emergency so keep this money separate from everything else.

And by emergency, I mean urgent house repairs, car repairs or medical bills – things that are genuinely unplanned (there is a difference, for instance, between an unexpected job loss and leaving a job you no longer like). You can even split your emergency fund into those different categories, as this can heighten the need to fund it and keep you reviewing your priorities.

I like to think of my emergency fund as my insurance fund. The difference is that I am in control of my expenses.

Santis O'Garro

The importance of having an emergency fund

No one has 100 per cent control over their lives but having a small amount of money put aside can alleviate the stress of coping with the different circumstances that life throws at us. The comfort of having an emergency fund relieves pressure, allowing us to think clearly and approach each problem with focus, helping us to solve it rather than feeling overwhelmed by it. Having an emergency fund is the difference between something going wrong really affecting your headspace and it being just a minor inconvenience.

I was lucky that, when my apartment flooded in 2018, I had home insurance in place that meant I was able to afford the necessary repairs. But what if I hadn't? I had been plunged into panic mode as it was, and I can't help thinking that I would have had clarity about the whole situation and been much calmer if I'd had an emergency fund in place. So, when I decided to take control of my finances, my first goal, before paying off any debts, was to save a €1,000 emergency fund. And boy was I happy that I did.

Three months later, and all within the same week, my boiler broke down, my washing machine decided that it had had its last spin, and a stone smashed my windscreen. All expensive to fix, and I was only just beginning to pay off my debt. I may have felt like I was living in an episode of *Fawlty Towers*, but thanks to my emergency fund, I could smile with relief knowing that it could've been worse. I could sit down and rationalise how, and within what time scale, I could fix things:

1. The insurance company could fix my car, but the glass company they suggested was charging €525. My excess was set at €350, so it would take €350 of my emergency fund in total. I decided to ring around to source my own repair company, and their charge was **€150**. That was €200 saved right there.
2. I was able to get the boiler fixed the very next day for a cost of **€150**.
3. Fixing the washing machine cost **€100**.

In the end this meant that I was able to get everything fixed at a cost of €400, and I wasn't worried because I had my €1,000 emergency fund. I was able to cover the cost of everything.

But suppose just one of these things had happened even just three months before. I *know* that I would have had a life-altering emotional breakdown. But instead, I was able to reason. Of course, it meant I had to pause my debt repayment to refill the pot, but I was delighted to do so because this was a first-hand example of how I was going about this the right way.

And the thing is, you are likely to find that you experience fewer emergencies once you have saved your emergency fund, because you are now in a place of awareness and organisation. You become much more aware of what could be a potential emergency, so you are more likely to take pre-emptive action. For example, you know it is likely that your car will break down at some point, so you may decide to include within your budget the cost of putting it through a yearly service to reduce the chances of anything happening;

or you decide to get health insurance rather than waiting for a health crisis. When you're budgeting and planning, disasters strikes less frequently as you are more proactive in dealing with financial issues before they become financial emergencies.

That's the thing with budgeting. *You might think you are only sorting out your money, but you're also developing the tools to build confidence in yourself.* A solid foundation leads to a solid structure.

How much should be in an emergency fund?

This depends on your circumstances, but my rule of thumb is that, if you are at the beginning of your journey, or if you are in debt, that before you start *overpaying* debt, you should have a fund equivalent to one month's expenses for both your Wall and Long Family costs (see Chapter 3 for more on this). Broken down, this comprises one month's total expenses for utilities, food, transport, housing, bill repayments, minimum debt repayments, savings and future planned expenses.

Financial advisors suggest that you aim for three months of expenses in your emergency fund, but I would go one further: have one year's income saved for an emergency. It might seem like an impossible task initially, but it is achievable. Save aggressively for your first three months and make saving towards your one-year emergency fund a continuous process. Again, this might seem overly cautious, but peace of mind is the game's name here.

And *if you are in a situation where you have been clearing your debts, and an emergency arises, then all extra debt payments should be paused.* Instead, your focus should be on refilling your emergency fund.

At the start of my debt-free journey, I followed budgeter Dave Ramsey's 'Baby Steps' plan, and worked towards saving €1000 as an emergency fund. However, I have since found that there is no 'one figure fits all' and this should be tailored to each household. Did you know that almost half of the people of Ireland are just three paydays away from relative poverty? That is why, instead of setting a number, I think the best approach is to look at your own expenses and build up enough of a cushion to cover a month's worth of outgoings instead. For instance, my mortgage was €1,150 per month, but I had only €1,000 saved. If something drastic had happened, I wouldn't have had enough to cover that essential expense. I was lucky that nothing happened that cost me more than €1,000.

Building an emergency fund – the stepping stones

It was the realisation that my emergency fund would not even cover my mortgage that led me to come up with my own journey plan, **THE STEPPING STONES**, which encourages followers to tailor their financial journey to their circumstances. To begin building your own emergency fund, I recommend following these steps (where possible and achievable):

STEP 1: Save one month's worth of Wall and Long Family expenses (including setting up your sinking funds). Try keeping some of this in cash in a safe place and the rest in an easily accessible current account.

STEP 2: Clear all debts. Then breathe, take time to reflect on what you have achieved. At this point on your journey, you may not yet be adept at budgeting, but you are maintaining your newfound habits.

STEP 3: Commit to increasing the amount in your emergency fund. Aim for six months' worth of expenses from all of the Four Families. Saving bonds can be good for this as you can withdraw the money, but it is not easily accessible.

STEP 4: Save a deposit for a mortgage if applicable.

STEP 5: Set up a fund for your children's future and commit to saving a small amount each payday.

STEP 6: Continue to fill emergency funds until you have a year's worth of all Four Family expenses saved.

STEP 7: Start planning for your future and investing.

STEP 8: Build wealth. If you haven't started your investment journey, then now is the time to consider it.

*Then breathe, and reflect – keep budgeting, but
don't feel that you have to climb towards a goal
aggressively. Instead, take this time to reflect
on where you are on your financial journey.*

I have found it's essential to stop and pause after reaching every life-changing landmark. This is a journey, and along the way it is vital to pat yourself on the back and reflect on how far you have come. It is also necessary to adjust along the way to suit your situation. For example, if you don't have children, building wealth and investing for your future might be a priority. Or maybe you are not interested in being wealthy (I was conscious about adding this step).

I achieved steps 1 and 2 quickly, and I am currently saving for step 4, although with inflation at an unbelievable rate of growth and house prices nearly unachievable, the main focus of my stepping stones journey is to give my children an education and a helping hand.

Another practical way to save for and organise your emergency fund is to save enough **to cover certain areas of your budget**. I would start by having enough to cover the Wall Family, so your essential needs:

- mortgage/rent
- utilities
- food shop
- transport
- childcare

Aim to have enough to pay your mortgage or rent one month in advance. Then when you have that, save enough to cover utilities, then petrol/bus fare. These are your basics, and it makes for a no-frills emergency fund. Sometimes numbers can be intimidating, and this is a great way to make the concept real and create an attachment to what you want. It is the perfect starting point.

Once you have one month's savings, work your way up to three months, and so on.

You should constantly be motivated to review your budget, but no matter what way you pay into and structure your emergency fund, make sure to keep it as a constant category within that budget. Although you might focus on another goal, you should always allow for some money to feed into that fund.

What is a saving fund?

So while an emergency fund is there to help you *just in case*, a sinking fund is a pot of money you save to put towards **PLANNED EXPENSES** or a particular saving goal.

Saving money can be tedious. It can feel that you're taking money out of your account for no other reason than to watch it pile up, so the temptation is always there to dip in at any time and have a splurge. A saving fund, however, has a **SET PURPOSE** – you know what you are saving that money for, and that it can only be taken back out for that particular purpose. Things like:

- pension
- holidays
- new kitchen appliances
- your child's college fees
- back-to-school expenses
- Christmas
- birthdays

You know you'll need to spend for these (birthdays are always going to happen), so why not be ready? Let's face it, *these expenses will come out of your budget whether you are prepared for them or not. The question is, where will that money be coming from?* We may have our emergency fund safely tucked away, but before we know it, Christmas is here and we have nothing saved. So, what do we do? We dip into that emergency fund; or we apply for a loan; or we might even pop it on the credit card. All of these things keep us trapped in the cycle of living payday to payday. But, if you work sinking funds into your budget, you can leave survival mode and move on to have a successful season.

Sinking funds are such a positive saving habit, and they really promote saving with intention. They can:

- enable you to break significant expenses into achievable goals;
- give you an overall picture of your annual saving goals;
- create awareness of what needs to be prioritised in your life;

- give you a positive outlook on your budgeting journey;
- help you stay organised and plan ahead;
- save you money (for instance, you can pay for something upfront instead of in inflated monthly instalments);
- offer peace of mind when you need to make big purchases as you know you already have the money in hand;
- make you more respectful of your own time and money – it's only when we start to save that we start to appreciate the effort it took to make that money in the first place;
- creates a great mindset towards savings.

When I started my debt payoff, there was one repayment that annoyed me: my car insurance. Of course, all of my repayments were frustrating, but that payment was particularly annoying. Back then my insurance was €723 per year, but I did not have the money to pay this bill in full, so I had to pay monthly. The monthly rate, however, was €65 per month, which worked out at a total of €780, so paying it this way cost me an extra €57 a year.

That may not seem like a lot, but that was money that could have been put to good use somewhere else: that was a third of my yearly car tax bill; that was three hours of me working in a job I did not like. The extra I had to pay meant I was missing other payments as I was under financial pressure every month.

By this point, I was paying nearly double my car payment. I felt trapped, and it made me associate my car, and my money in general, with stress. I was paying for the privilege of driving a car, yet the repayments ruined my experience.

When I decided to start a sinking fund for my car insurance, I put away €13.50 every week until I had €700. For me, this was so tough, but only for that first year as the following year when my car insurance payment was due, I was able to pay it in full. That year, the difference between paying it in full (€596) and paying monthly (€59, meaning an annual sum of €708), meant a difference in repayment of €112.

If I'd had to pay the €59 per month, it would have brought me over that €700 budget. Instead, the €104 that I had left still in the fund went towards the following year's car insurance sinking fund, which meant I could fill that one even more quickly. Or, instead of needing to save €13.50 per week, I could reduce that to €11.50 and still reach my €700 target in time, while that €2 I saved every week could go towards another sinking fund.

I now had choices.

This, along with the one for my car tax, is one of my favourite sinking funds as it makes me feel very proud of how far I have come.

Getting started with saving funds

The good news is that it's likely you already have experience of saving for a saving fund – if you have ever saved towards anything, let's say a holiday, then you have already been practising for this!

If you want to fine-tune the process, I would say to organise your saving funds in categories depending on:

- importance
- amount needed
- time available
- where you save them

I like to group my saving funds based on the time I have available before I will need the money and by what is the most important. I group them into three categories:

- short-term saving funds (car insurance, Christmas, bills);
- medium-term saving funds (dream holiday, household appliances);
- long-term saving fund (kids' college);

As to the where, depending on the type of saving fund, you can avail of many different saving methods and locations. Keeping your fund in **cash via cash envelopes** can be a great starter as a way to keep you motivated, though this would be most suitable for short-term saving funds. For longer-term savings, you might consider **neobanks** (also known as an online-only or internet-only banks), which have vaults where you can customise the amount you need to save, or even just a simple **savings account** would do.

How do I calculate my saving funds?

For me, the simplest and most effective way to calculate how much you will need per sinking fund is to **SPLIT AND GO**: you estimate how much something is going to cost and divide the total by the number of paydays between now and when you'll need the money. That will be the amount you need to put away for that saving fund each payday.

For example, say you were saving for a Christmas sinking fund:

- Make a list of those you are shopping for;
- Note how much you want to spend on each person and add it all together;
- Add the cost of the Christmas food shop and whatever else you tend to buy for the festivities;
- Then divide the total by the number of paydays between now and Christmas.

Always consider the lifestyle and extra expenses that come with having this new goal. If we stick with Christmas as the example, then you need to remember that other expenses will crop up at that time of year – you need to be saving for a lot more than gifts in December.

If you find that the amount is too high, then it is time to make some decisions: Can I reduce the cost allocated to presents? Can I commit to cutting back on my food budget during the year so I can put more towards my Christmas saving fund? Can I find a way to earn extra income?

How about another example? This time, a house saving fund.

If you are a homeowner, you know how annoying it is when something goes wrong. A run of broken appliances, for instance, could have you reaching for your emergency fund or your home insurance. But if you were prepared – especially if it was to fix or replace something that you knew would eventually need to be replaced – you can transition out from needing to dip into your emergency fund to accessing your saving fund instead. (You can also use this method for bigger repairs in the house.)

You don't need to look at everything, but have a think about some appliances that you think would eventually need replacing:

- What appliances would need to be replaced in the next five years?
- Put a value on the estimated costs and divide this number by five (for each year).
- If you get paid weekly, divide that new amount by fifty-two; or if monthly, divide by twelve.
- Then save that amount every payday.

How you then choose to approach saving for the saving fund is up to you, but no matter your budget, you should have room for saving funds within it.

If you have the income, for instance, you could save for all of your saving funds at once. So, for example, if you have nine different things that you want to put money away for, and that comes to a total of €45, then every week you send €45 to all of those funds.

If that is not possible, then focus on filling one fund at a time. As you might recall from earlier in the book, I call this **THE SNOWBALL METHOD**. To work out which fund to prioritise, list out all of your sinking funds, calculate how much you need to set aside for each, then consider:

- What is due first?
- What is the most significant amount?
- What is the smallest amount?

If you are only new to saving, I would suggest you tackle the smallest amount first as this creates momentum (the satisfaction of completely filling one sinking fund will encourage you to move on to the next, and the next, and the next – hence the snowball). However, it is up to you – you may need to prioritise based on due date first.

Personal finances are just that – personal. So it is really up to you how and what you want to save towards and how you do it; as long as it is working for you in your household, that's all that matters. And how empowering it is to be able to make decisions *right now* that your future self would thank you for. That is the power of saving funds.

Mentor's Notes

- Having an emergency fund is the safety net you need to stop an inconvenience becoming a crisis.
- Saving funds will enable you to cover costs you know are looming.
- Having both is crucial to financial health.

To recap . . .

To start your journey towards financial wellness.

- You need to have a plan of action, **a financial plan**, in place.
- To ensure that your money knows where it needs to go, you need a **budget.**
- You need to have an **emergency fund** and **saving funds** in place.
- You need to start **clearing your debt** to become less reliant on credit.
- You must start **talking openly** about money.
- You should start to read books about money – **financial literacy** is so critical.
- You should try to find a **mentor**; this could be someone you follow on the internet or someone you respect in real life.

MONEY AND MODERN LIVING

CHAPTER 6:

STATE BENEFITS

Attitudes towards state benefits and social welfare

There is a stigma in Ireland when it comes to receiving state benefits or social welfare, which leads to a sense of deep-rooted shame in the recipients. We can work and make state contributions all our lives, but when it's time to receive, we are made to feel unworthy. I don't know where this attitude came from, but I know that it's something that I have experienced directly.

I have always been a grafter. I've always worked hard in every job I've ever had and pushed myself to excel at what I do. For seventeen years, I worked full-time in a bookmaker (aka 'the bookies') and in 2019, I decided to go part-time. I had been writing for *Irish Country Magazine* and I had received a small inheritance from my grandfather, so the time felt right. I thought this would give me the best of both worlds.

However, in 2020, during the Black Lives Matter movement, and as the world was beginning to open up again after the pandemic, I started to have severe panic attacks. These were not new, but they came back with a bang. If you have ever been in a bookies, you'll maybe appreciate that, while it can be a gratifying job, even at the best of times it can be a hostile environment. I had already had people spit on me, call me names and abuse me on the street. One customer had even threatened to burn my kids from a car, and the thought of having to experience that for the rest of my working life was just not appealing. As my counsellor says, I was conditioned to that environment because everybody accepted it as usual, and, up to that point, I had not made a formal complaint for fear of being an inconvenience, but I wasn't willing to accept it anymore. I decided that I would do anything rather than go back to my job.

I pushed my business, and I invested in myself. I became a qualified coach, and I developed a budget mindset planner that I sold through my website. The planners sold out in six weeks, but I soon realised that running a business was perhaps more complicated than I thought – my outgoings were higher than my incomings, and I realised that I wasn't earning enough to feed my family.

If I had known better, or was more familiar with the social welfare system, I could have taken time out of the bookies on sick pay, because it wasn't my fault that I was in a situation where my family and I had been threatened. Instead, in 2021, I was fully assessed to be subsidised with the One-Parent Family Payment (OFP). It was so hard for me to admit that my income needed to be supplemented. Throughout my whole life, I have never taken sick pay. I had never even thought of social welfare, and here I was now having to, in my opinion, beg for help. I was so embarrassed, and the social welfare officer knew it. But that kind of thinking is wrong.

Even now, though I feel justified to be able to receive social welfare, I still feel I must explain my situation so that people do not judge me. But and I want to make this clear, I'm no longer talking about this from a place of *embarrassment*.

The Irish welfare system is one of the best globally, it was created to help people like me who genuinely need the extra income to live day to day. We should be so proud that we have a system built to help our low-income earners live ordinary lives. Some countries don't have it as an option, and have huge issues with extreme poverty. Instead, we judge each other and ourselves, but just because you need to claim state benefits does not mean that you are lazy, trying to rip off the system, or expecting 'handouts' from our government: instead, you are using a system developed for people in situations where their income does not meet their needs. I wouldn't be so naive as to say that *nobody* on social welfare is bleeding the system, but it annoys me when I hear people say, 'Go and get a job,' when they see a particular demographic of people claiming state benefits (that is why people don't admit to claiming them – they don't want to get tarred with the same brush). I find that often, the people who complain about those claiming social welfare are the same people who praise the wealthiest in society for avoiding paying their taxes. It is food for thought.

I asked my Instagram followers to give me their honest thoughts on social welfare. My audience is primarily women, from low-income earners to high-income earners to retirees, and it was fascinating to see how everybody had a different take on this somewhat controversial topic. I received so many replies (all anonymous) that it took me four days to get through them all. I take the role of a money mentor rather seriously: people need to talk about their financial situations not just when they're winning, but when they're not. It often feels as though when I ask the hardest of questions, people use my comment box as an excuse to unload.

Here are some of the responses:

- 'It's a great support when used by people who genuinely need it.'
- 'I wouldn't have survived without it. My relationship broke down, and I was jobless with three young kids.'
- 'It's a sign that other systems have failed: education, housing or other supports.'
- 'The means tests make it unattractive to work more.'
- 'It's too easy in Ireland to abuse it, which creates the stigma.'
- 'I work full time, but I know people on social welfare that are better off than me and who've never worked a day in their life.'

What was clear is that there is a complicated range of opinions on the subject, ranging from genuine empathy to outright anger. Some people felt that their taxes were being mismanaged, and that claimants were taking advantage of the system – but what we must realise is that some people are born into that mindset: it's hard to beat that conditioning when this is the norm for your environment, and those who abuse the system are not necessarily winning. Others acknowledged that receiving social welfare can be a trap – as one of the responders put it, the means test makes it not worthwhile to work extra hours as, to stay within your subsidy you have to earn below a certain amount. This means putting a limit on yourself and your financial freedom. I think people have this idea that everyone claiming does so by choice. Which isn't always true.

As one responder put it, 'Being on long-term benefits can destroy you – very few people are on them long term because they are lazy. They are probably devoid of self-esteem because Irish society looks down their noses and treats them with disdain. People on benefits have a much lower outcome in their physical and mental health, housing education and life span.'

This country is self-judgemental, and people often suffer from a superiority complex when they have no right. Being viewed as financially successful is more important than having empathy for others and the class system developed to divide us – are you lower-income? middle class? high-earning? – is doing its job. But remember the saying: you need to walk a mile in someone else's shoes to see the truth.

Social welfare needs to be presented in a better light, both for those who claim it and those who need it. We have just come out of a pandemic, and we're facing rates of inflation that are higher than before. Benefits are there to help people who are struggling, and if they need to get financial support from the state, from a system that was put in place *for* them, they should not be ashamed. This is something that we as Irish citizens should celebrate and acknowledge: the system is in place to help people who don't have as much as you do, and it is a system that, one day, you yourself might need.

Applying for benefits and welfare

There are so many different types of welfare . . .

- supplements
- allowances
- pensions
- grants
- child benefit
- sick pay
- back-to-work schemes

. . . and to gain access, you must meet specific criteria. Some are simple, and some are more complicated. Most of the benefits can only be accessed if you have made PRSI contributions in the past; some are available to everybody, regardless of contributions. And the value of each benefit differs wildly. For instance, I get a subsidy with my pay to bring me up to the living rate, but I won't get as much as an eighteen-year-old on unemployment benefits.

It can all be a bit of a minefield, so here is some important information to help you out:

- There are two different types of social welfare: **BENEFITS** are based on your PRSI contributions; **SOCIAL WELFARE ASSISTANCE** is based on your means-test results.
- **MEANS TESTING** is where you declare all assets, savings and investments so that the social welfare office can calculate precisely how much you can be given.
- Not all social welfare benefits are tax-free. It doesn't depend on your income, so this is something that you should check.

Money is the last taboo, just as I mentioned earlier, so the idea of having to be accountable to a stranger can leave you feeling humiliated. Not only that, but before I made my claim, I had been told that the whole process was torture, and that the staff were incredibly strict. As one friend put it, 'You would swear the money was coming out of their own pockets.' I heard a lot of this, but I was pleasantly surprised that the lady who dealt with me was both compassionate and kind. As was one Instagram responder, who works in the social welfare office:

> I have been on the other side of the counter and know how daunting it can be to walk into the social welfare office. I would advise anyone on social welfare payments to speak with their local

case officer in the local Intreo office to avail of courses and schemes (such as the Back to Work Enterprise Allowance).

Like in all walks of life, you will meet people who are willing to help and people who do the bare minimum in their job, so your best bet is to be prepared. Make sure that you educate yourself on what exactly is available to you and your family by contacting www.mywelfare.ie and www.citizensinformation.ie.

Then, before you present your case to the social welfare office, make a list of exactly what you might need help with and have a list of the questions that you need answered. You'll want to have as much information to hand as you possibly can (what your income is, what your circumstances are, and so on), because this is a very busy department and sometimes it can be difficult getting through to speak to somebody.

What is a means test?
A means test checks if you have enough financial resources to support yourself and what amount of social assistance payment, if any, you might qualify for. In a means test, the Department of Social Protection (DSP) examines all your sources of income.

When you apply for a means-tested social welfare payment, you must fill out an application form. This form asks for information about sources of income. The DSP can ask you for details of your bank accounts, including account numbers. The DSP does not access your bank account unless you give them permission though. A social welfare inspector might want to interview you about your income and ask you for supporting documents, such as bank statements or accounts. Sometimes, this can involve a visit out to your home.

What benefits are out there?

The social welfare system, and even the names of the payments available, change all the time, but information on what's available to you is always only a few clicks away. Gathered here is some information on these resources, but you can find more through the Citizens Information website, which I would really advise as it's a great source of useful info. With this chapter of my book, I hope it might be a starting point in figuring out what is available to you and your family and how you can go about getting this help.

One-Parent Family (OPF)

The One-Parent Family Payment (OFP) is for men and women under the age of sixty-six who bring children up without a supporting partner. It's important to remember that to receive this payment, you will be means-tested. Your children must be under the age of seven for this benefit. You *can* work and get OFP, and the first €165 of your gross weekly earnings (wages and profit from self-employment) is not considered in the means test. However, half the remainder of your gross earnings per week is assessed as means, and you may get a reduced rate of OFP depending on how much you earn.

Back-to-work enterprise allowance

This allowance encourages people to get certain social welfare payments to become self-employed. If you participate in the scheme, you can keep some of your social welfare payment for two years. This payment is made by the Department of Social Protection (DSP) to people under the age of sixty-six.

Jobseeker's Allowance

One of the primary conditions for getting a Jobseeker's Allowance is that you must be unemployed. However, you do not have to be out of work – for four days out of seven consecutive days; you must be unemployed. Therefore, it is important you are available for and looking for work. You will be means tested on jobseeker's allowance, so your household income must be below a certain level to qualify.

Jobseeker's Benefit

You must also be free and ready to work looking for employment and meet all the others. In addition, you must have enough social insurance contributions.

Here are some conditions for getting Jobseeker's Benefit:

1. Reduced work days due to lack of work.
2. You are a part-time worker; this includes involuntary job-sharing week on and week off (but not if you have chosen to do so).
3. You get casual work or part-time work.
4. You have subsidiary employment.

One of the primary conditions for getting Jobseeker's Benefit is that you must be unemployed. However, you do not have to be out of work – for at least four days out of the seven-day social welfare employment week. Although a Jobseeker's Allowance is tested, the Jobseeker's Benefit is not.

Working Family Payment (WFP)

This is a weekly tax-free payment for employed people with children. It is specifically for people who are on a low income. Working Family Payment (WFP) used to be called Family Income Supplement (FIS). You have to be employed to get this payment and you cannot qualify if you are self-employed only. You should be financially supporting at least one child who lives with you.

I have had so many parents tell me of the relief they have felt when they no longer needed to worry about back-to-school expenses. One mother told me summertime had been a time of dread for nineteen years as she found it so stressful to think about the costs of going back to school. This chapter is about state benefits, but it is also an opportunity to discuss back-to-school costs and those costs associated with raising our children. It affects me, and I have had to adapt myself, my finances and my lifestyle to meet the cost of raising children.

In an ideal world, the correct way to have children is to plan ahead before we take the plunge, so we can be financially secure and can provide our children with a great life. However, as we well know, life happens and having children can be an emotional decision more than anything else – and sometimes it's not a decision at all. One thing that is certain is that children are expensive – but the important thing to remember is, there is help out there.

Below, I've laid out some of the state benefits to help with raising our kids:

Child Benefit

To avail of the Child Benefit monthly payment, you must be parents or guardians of children under the age of sixteen. You can get Child Benefit for children aged sixteen and seventeen if they are in full-time education or training, or have a disability and cannot support themselves. Child Benefit is not paid for any children aged eighteen or older, even if they are in full-time education or training.

Maternity Benefit

Maternity Benefit is a payment made to women on maternity leave from work and covered by social insurance (PRSI). You should apply for Maternity Benefit at least six weeks before you plan to go on maternity leave. To get Maternity Benefit, you must have a certain number of paid PRSI contributions and be in insurable employment up to the first day of your maternity leave. After that, your PRSI contributions can be from employment or self-employment.

The National Childcare Scheme (NCS)

This scheme exists to help parents meet childcare costs. The NCS provides two types of childcare subsidies for children aged over six months and up to fifteen (children aged fifteen don't qualify though – it was only recently extended to children aged up to fifteen in 2022.). This subsidy is not means-tested.

Back-to-School Clothing and Footwear Allowance (BTSCFA)

The Back-to-School Clothing and Footwear Allowance (BTSCFA) helps you meet the cost of uniforms and footwear for children. This allowance is a life-saver for many parents, and you can apply for it online.

Medical Card

To qualify for a medical card, your weekly income must be below a specific amount in relation to your family size. Cash income, savings, investments and property (except for your own home) are considered in the means test.

GP Visit Card

For whatever reasons, you may not qualify for a medical card. However, you may be eligible for a GP visit card. A GP visit card allows you to visit a participating GP for free. To qualify for a GP visit card, you must meet the eligibility rules, which you can find through citizens' information, and be living in Ireland for at least one year.

Drugs Payment Scheme

Through this scheme, you and your family only have to pay a maximum of €80 each month for approved prescribed drugs, medicines and some appliances. This scheme covers you, your spouse or partner, your children if they are aged under eighteen (or under twenty-three if in full-time education) or a family member with a physical or intellectual disability or mental illness that means they cannot fully look after themselves. In the latter case, you need to include a medical report for the family member who cannot maintain themselves.

Carer's Benefit

Carer's Benefit is paid to people who leave work or reduce their hours to care for a person needing full-time care. You can avail of the Carer's Benefit for two years for each person you care for. However, if you interrupt your Carer's Benefit claim for less than six weeks in a row, you will have to wait another six weeks before you can get Carer's Benefit for the same person again.

Disability Allowance

Disability Allowance (DA) is paid weekly to people with a disability. You can get DA from the age of sixteen, and you can get DA even if you are still in school. However, your doctor must complete a report on your medical condition as part of the application form. This report is reviewed by one of the Department of Social Protection's medical assessors.

These are just a few examples of what is available, and I have only touched on them in light detail here, but for more detailed information, do go to the Citizens Information website, or give them a call. It can be intimidating, but **THEY ARE THERE TO HELP**.

Many of us are entitled to so many welfare payments that we aren't aware of. Some of these benefits are taxable, and some are not. Many are based on your PRSI contributions, and many are means-tested.

Social welfare and state benefits are there for a purpose. Use them as much as you need but try to always look at the bigger picture, which is financial freedom. It can be very hard and for some people it isn't an option, but what I would say is, before you get too deep into the cycle, look at ways of raising your income elsewhere.

Mentor's Notes
- We all need to be a bit more tolerant and non-judgemental when it comes to claiming benefits.
- The system is there to help you if you need it.
- Do your research and find out what you are entitled to.

CHAPTER 7:

EMPLOYMENT AND SIDE HUSTLES

To anyone about to get your first job, I'd like to say that this will be the most significant pay rise of your life. You've probably never had so much money at once before and it can be all too easy to get carried away with those hard-earned wages just burning a hole in your pocket!

For the rest of us 'seasoned' employees, we all know by now that sometimes the money we make just isn't stretching far enough. So, it's no surprise that one of the most common questions I get asked is, 'How do I earn extra money?'

I have many followers who are savvy savers and are good with money, yet they have already squeezed every saving they can through budgeting. So sometimes, the best option for them is to try and increase their income.

Easier said than done, right? Well, that's what this chapter is all about . . .

Asking for a raise

So, first of all, are you being paid fairly for your role?

Nobody in their right mind wants to be underpaid, but

we exist in a culture that seems to frown upon those who talk openly about their salaries, which makes it tough to know exactly how much your colleagues are getting paid in similar positions. While employers should be forthcoming about paying employees fairly, it falls to the employee to be assertive about their salary in order to increase their wages.

This, unfortunately, is a particularly pressing issue for women in the workplace. There has been a lot of open discussion in recent years about the gender pay gap that exists within most occupations, and there have been developments such as the Gender Pay Gap Information Act 2021, which requires larger organisations (those with over 250 employees) to report on their gender pay gap, bonus pay and the proportions of males and females in lower-middle, upper-middle and important quality roles. However, even with all the media coverage, there is still a considerable gap between women and men in the same workplace positions. Many women find that their male counterparts have negotiated a higher salary before even starting their roles, and men tend to ask for more pay rises.

In my opinion, there are a lot of talented women who just don't know their worth and so tend to devalue their workplace contributions. Many of us are so used to critiquing ourselves and pinpointing our deficiencies that we do not celebrate what we do well.

So I'm saying that if you *want* a pay rise, if you *deserve* a pay rise, if you *need* a pay rise, you have to ask. So I want to give you some tools to help you approach your company or organisation:

- **Stop trying to be a perfectionist in the role that you have now. Instead, try to acquire the skills for the role you want.** If you become too good at one role, you become indispensable. This means it wouldn't be in your employer's best interest to move you up.
- **Impostor syndrome hits us all,** and it hinders many women. So make sure you celebrate your wins no matter how small they are, and challenge those feelings when they come to you. Don't allow anyone, including yourself, to tell you that you can't do something.
- **Stop focusing on past mistakes.** Sometimes we hinder ourselves by focusing on things that we didn't do the way we wanted to. If you're not in the present, you should be planning for the future. Women can often be guilty of rumination, where we internalise our mistakes. This can lead to counterproductivity, as our sole focus is on all the small mistakes that we've made, so we find it impossible to go forward.
- **Make sure that you record your achievements and contributions to the team.** Be prepared to present this to your boss when negotiating a pay rise. Show up with confidence because now you are showing your worth.
- **Be prepared to be hyper-focused and stop trying to please everybody**. Focus on the task at hand, do the work to back it up, and don't be afraid to ask for what you need.
- **Maintain good relationships with the people you work with, and network with the right ones to get ahead.** Remember, you are the company you keep.
- **Check your company's pay bands and see where you fall on the scale.** Is this in line with your

experience and performance? Some websites, such as Glassdoor, also give a benchmark.

- **Check what you could be paid in another role if vacancies are free.**
- **Calculate whether the perks might be worth more than your gross pay.** Make sure you sit down with a pen and paper and work out the pros and cons of staying vs moving on. Think about non-financial incentives, such as working from home (WFH) in a lower-paid role, which helps reduce the cost of childcare, vs moving to a better-paid role where there is no flexibility.
- **Be prepared to walk away from your current role if you don't get a pay rise . . .**
- **. . . or look at your current job with fresh eyes.** The time might not be suitable for you to move to another job, but what are you learning here? Where else can you apply these learnings? If your job is skilled, could you create a side hustle with your knowledge?

When you decide to have the conversation with the person who pays you, say to yourself that you need to act today. Set up the meeting there and then, so you get the fear and you know that you need to start prepping. Then, 1-2-3, write that email and send it. You are allowed to ask.

And when you are in the meeting, focus on what you bring to the business rather than saying things like 'I need more money.' (You'd be surprised how many people do this).

Instead, focus on saying, 'My performance has resulted in XYZ, and therefore I feel that I deserve a pay rise that recognises that contribution.'

Side hustles

I'm all about side hustles – also known as doing 'nixers' or moonlighting – but nothing about them is easy. Even the term side hustle (which is an American phrase) gets a bad rep because it contains the word 'hustle', and we equate that with doing something underhanded or behind someone's back, but it isn't. It is simply a means of earning money on top of your regular income or day job, therefore a way to elevate your earnings.

It is also a way to establish a little financial security as, currently, it is wise to have multiple income streams. During the last recession and during the lockdown, many people lost their jobs and their power to earn, but even without those extreme circumstances, job security is still a thing of the past. There is a timeline when you work for a company, and many ways that your term of employment can come to an end: the company could be dissolved, you could get fired or made redundant, new technology may make your role obsolete, or you could just choose to retire. But when you create multiple income streams, the stress of losing one job is lessened – you always have other sources of income to fall back on.

I believe depending on one source of income is the riskiest path to go down. As a single mother living in a house with one income, I needed to stay loyal to my budget and to always have a backup. So instead of just earning an extra income, I wanted to make sure that I had other income streams, so if something should go wrong with one job, I would always have something else to fall back on.

At the time of writing:
- I am a regular columnist for a magazine, and I get paid as a freelancer
- I do brand advertisements on my social media streams
- I make money through affiliate links to products and services I endorse and use myself
- I am a public speaker and panellist
- I run educational workshops for businesses and schools
- I'm a TV presenter on a prime-time TV show
- I sell products like cash-saving envelopes, budget planners and stationery through my website, the budgetmindsetclub.com
- I write a blog on TheCaribbeanDub.com
- I run a YouTube channel
- I host a weekly workshop service where I speak openly about money (courses.budgetmindsetclub.com)
- I also do surveys and mystery shopping.

I don't list all of these to show off or brag, but to show you what is possible. Yes, I'm aware this is a lot for any human being, but these activities are part of my business and they're all intricately linked. I also see them as an investment of my time – my numerous side hustles have turned into my real hustle, my primary source of income.

Most of us are romantic, and we believe that if we just follow our passions or dreams, or if we do something on the side straight away, we can leave our jobs and start a whole new life for ourselves . . . but that often isn't the case. Committing to a side hustle takes a lot of prep work, effort and planning to get started.

When I first thought about money-mentoring as a side hustle I followed my passion, which was talking and writing about money, and I shared everything I learned on my social media channels, but I did this while I was still working in full-time, then part-time employment and even then, it was a lot of hard work. Unfortunately, I see so many people jumping in at the deep end. They don't take the time to appreciate the long-term implications of committing to what is essentially another job. If people are paying you for them, they will expect your goods/services to be of high quality. This often leads to burnout and landing back at square one financially.

It is a great idea to earn money on the side for many different reasons, depending on the time or the energy you have to devote to it, but more than anything, a side hustle can be a game-changer for your finances . . . *if* you approach it sensibly. So aim to choose a side hustle that suits your resources and is worth your time and energy.

Choosing a side hustle

Although the thought of earning extra money can be tempting, taking on more work can be daunting, especially if you're already time-poor, so a side hustle should reflect the time you know you have. Before you commit to anything, think long-term and be realistic about how much of your resources, such as your time and your energy, you can commit to side-hustling.

It is heartbreaking to see people give up on their budgeting journey because they took on a side hustle (which is essentially another job) and ended up feeling burnt out. So the best way to approach a side hustle is to **start where you are right now** and consider ways to earn extra income within the job you are currently doing. It is an excellent strategy for people who don't necessarily want to change or commit to another working environment.

Look at your current job with fresh eyes and try to make yourself available for internal opportunities: Is there overtime on offer? Where are you on your company's pay scale? Is there a promotion coming up?

And if opportunities in your workplace are limited, *then* look to your own skills. **What can you do that you can make money from?** Get a piece of paper and list out skills that you have: maybe you're a fast typer; quick and efficient at creating websites; an amateur photographer; a teacher; good with Microsoft Word, Excel or PowerPoint; a writer; a graphic designer . . . the list goes on. If you are good at it, if you are working in an industry that hones your skills, or if it's something that's a real hobby and a passion for you, then put it on your list. And when you've mapped out exactly what your skills are and what you're good at, you need to sit down and figure out how this skill can make you money. For instance, there are sites such as Fiverr and Freelancer where you can advertise your services, and find clients who will pay you for them.

This is also the time to put some serious thought into something you would love to do, such as a hobby, then try and come up with ways you can monetise it. Log on to freelance sites and see what people might want. If you love animals, you can take up dog-walking or even dog-sitting (some people pay up to €100 a day to have someone look after their canine). Or if you are obsessed with cleaning and have a tip for everything, that is a service you can offer. Not just as a cleaner but also in a less hands-on way – maybe by creating an automated service on the likes of Etsy and Shopify where you can sell printables of your cleaning tips and tricks. Once you have set these up, you can let them run on with very little ongoing maintenance needed.

You have here an opportunity to earn money around *your* lifestyle. There is no 'one-size-fits-all' scenario, and how you would earn money depends on your skills, the time and energy you have to dedicate to it, your interests, and the opportunities you can create. Only you know what these things are. And remember, it is not always about just making money, it's about making money on *your* terms. You might already have a job where you work for somebody else, and you're doing that on their terms.

I have worked in retail environments since I was twelve. I knew my skills were centred around customer service: I'm a natural chatterbox, I get value from helping others, and I'm an empath. I'm very emotionally led and I love to write, so talking and writing about money from an emotional viewpoint came naturally to me.

As I searched for new ways of paying off debt and saving money, I shared much of my story on Instagram. Talking about money isn't sexy, but it is practical and needed, so I shared freely without wanting anything back except accountability. I didn't know much about social media and for the longest time, I didn't realise that people were practising what I was sharing and making changes in their own lives. But as the number of followers I had began to grow – someone was now watching, and someone was noticing – I realised that I had become something of a money blogger and an influencer, and over time, I created more ways to communicate my message.

I hadn't realised that simply talking about money could generate an income. Instead, my side hustles came about organically – from a place of need rather than a long-term goal. I had been seeking a hobby and an outlet, but fast-forward a few years and I was now running ahead to keep up with everything available to me. Just by being honest about how I had improved my finances, and using my ability to engage with large audiences, I found a side hustle I enjoyed and that others got value from, too. I had something created from the skills I had, the interests that I shared with others, and the opportunities available to me.

So take your time; do your research; find something that works best for you. And in the meantime, here are some of my suggestions for making extra money:

- **Rent out your spare room:** If you have a spare bedroom, you should consider doing this – I have known people who have paid for holidays and house renovations by taking in lodgers. For several years I rented my spare bedroom to international students, all of whom were respectful and who ended up feeling like members of the family. You really can't just do this for the money, though, as it can be a complicated process to have a stranger share your personal space. As much as you might want to become territorial, you're being paid good money to make someone feel welcome. Just make sure to set boundaries in place that will benefit both you and your tenants, especially for international students. I want them to remember Ireland as a great country and I feel kindness plays a huge role in that.
- **Become a mystery shopper:** If you are on the shy side, then this may not suit, but if you fancy yourself as a bit of a Magnum PI, then this is for you. Mystery shopping is a decent way to earn some money on the side.
- **Surveys**: I find surveys interesting, but they can be very time consuming. Still, some offer money for completing them, and some surveys have affiliate links (so I share my link, and every time someone does a

survey, I get 10 per cent of what they earn). I can get on average €1.50 a day just from the links I have shared).

- **Sell second-hand products:** I realised this was lucrative when I started selling through channels such as the Facebook marketplace. I know people who can spin a decent sale from items bought in second-hand shops.

Google has many suggestions for ways to make money from home, and this will continue to evolve, as will the job market out there. Just make sure that, whatever side hustles you sign up to, they are ethical and authentic to who you are. I know many influencers who signed up for everything just because they focus on the money, but the money will come if you stay loyal to *you*.

Tips on how to hustle

So now that you've decided what your side hustle will be, you might be interested in some of my thoughts and tips on the process!

- **Do your research:** is there a market for the service you are offering? Who are your competitors? What are they doing?
- **Put a plan in place:** it is important to know what you want to get out of this
- **But stop and take stock from time to time**: analyse the pros and cons and revise them as you go.

- **Prepare for imposter syndrome:** starting any new venture can be difficult, and it is only natural to have periods of self-doubt. Just remember you chose this side hustle for a reason. You have skills and you have abilities, and now you're just showing them off to the world!

- **Give yourself a timeline to be up and running:** figure out the amount of time you will need to get your hustle up and running and work towards that as a launch date. It will keep you motivated and on track.

- **Set time aside:** it can be hard to dedicate time to creating a new side hustle, and I've heard so many people say, 'You need to give up your Saturdays; you need to give up every night; you need to get up early in the morning.' But everybody's situation is different. I can't tell you exactly how much time you need to dedicate to your side hustle, but a good starting point is four hours per week.

- **Discuss it with family and friends:** have an honest conversation to let them know precisely why you are taking this valuable time away from them. Explain that this will be good for everybody and outline the sacrifices it will take.

- **Create boundaries** both with yourself and others. If people see that you are good at something, they will bombard you with requests. If this is the case, my two top tips are: Up your prices or increase production – demand is clearly much higher than supply. Create a priority list – who are your best-paying, or best to work for, customers?

- **Be goal- and time-specific:** This is your second job, so treat it accordingly. Give yourself deadlines and hold yourself accountable if you miss them. The time you dedicate to creating this extra income should be taken as seriously as when you go to work. So get a quiet place, get into the zone, get your head down, and work.
- **Set financial goals** – how much would you like to make from this?
- **Keep financial records**: keep all of your receipts regarding the business and claim any expenses against tax.

I left this point to last as many people tend worry about the salary and tax implications of taking on another revenue stream – and yes, you must declare any extra income that you earn as revenue.

People fear the taxman, but there is no need to. Clarify how much tax you should be paying, or even if you need to be paying taxes at all, by logging on to www.revenue.ie and get the answers from the horse's mouth. It may, for instance, be possible to pay the tax due on your sideline business via your PAYE job (if the profit for your business is less than €5,000 per year and your gross income is less than €30,000). If you receive over €5,000 however, you must register to be self-assessed.

Do your best to try and understand precisely how the tax band works, and if in doubt, give them a call and speak to an advisor. They won't bite!

Freelancing

It may be the case that your side hustle (or maybe even your full-time job) involves freelancing.

I have been working as a freelancer for the last two years, and I have learned a lot in that time. I have been in positions where I've been valued, undervalued, or even taken advantage of. I feel this is a whole other conversation that needs to happen and as women, we tend not to share. But I feel that to share and disclose creates an honesty where we all profit.

So, with that in mind, I wanted to share those tips that I practice as both a freelancer and self-employed business owner. I've picked these from conversations with financial planners, financial advertisers and freelancer friends who have a lot more experience than I do:

- **Create a media kit or a price list depending on what industry you're in.** This shows that you know your work, know what you're capable of, have clear boundaries around pricing, and tells future employers precisely what you have on offer.
- **Make sure you include a timeframe for when you expect to be paid.** Some jobs that I did had a timeframe of 90 days, but this has never been a problem because I knew the arrangement upfront and so was able to plan for it. I was then aware of the importance of putting an acceptable payment window into my media kit.

- **Pay yourself a salary.** You need to look at your business as if it is a business that you work for; this creates a level of financial pressure and also makes you want to go and work hard so that you can pay yourself. This way you know straight away what is going towards your tax, what is going towards reinvesting, and what your profits are.
- **Outsource specific jobs if you can.** If you need someone to proofread what you've written or you need someone to take photos for an ad that you're doing, outsource it so you're getting the best quality for the job. This will earn you a lot more in the long run and shows your professionalism.

However you do it, it is possible to earn money on top of what you already bring in. Like all things, you just need to do your research, take your time, and find something that works for you.

Mentor's Notes
- Having multiple income streams offers peace of mind.
- If you plan to ask for a raise, make sure to put your case together before having the conversation.
- Try and limit your time at work where possible by creating passive streams of income.

CHAPTER 8:

GETTING THE MOST FROM FINANCIAL INSTITUTIONS

Let's face it, dealing with financial institutions can be daunting – from banks to insurance companies to credit unions, there's a lot to understand, but hopefully after this chapter, you'll come away with a better understanding of just how you can make these institutions work for you, and how you can make your money go further with them.

Banks will often offer attractive current accounts as a gateway to building customer loyalty, because in the future if you chose to take out a loan, you're more likely to go with the bank you have a current account with than one you don't. Most people don't shop around and tend to go with the most convenient option at the time, but there are lots of options out there, with other banks and also with your local credit union.

I am someone that has had always had a fond relation with the credit union. The credit union always seemed to me like the banks' nicer, more homely cousin, where low-income earners are welcome and given the chance of having a better life and of making our creature comforts more attainable.

What is a credit union?

Like your local GAA club, the credit union is a non-profit financial co-op owned by its members. If you have an account with your local credit union, you are a member. A credit union can be formed in different ways, based on where people work or even their locality. This is where they differ from banks. Profits that a credit union makes, or the surplus money it generates each year, are used to run the credit union, develop its services, give members dividends, or offer interest rebates to those with loans. A credit union's interest rates are also used to fund the loans offered to other members. Now, some credit unions don't give out dividends or interest rebates due to financial regulation – it's worth checking with your local branch if they do or not. One of the things that makes credit unions different from banks is that the services they provide differ from one credit union branch to another. This is because members of that credit union have the power to vote on how it is run.

Credit unions have a great reputation for a reason, as they were originally formed to help their members – regular people like you and me – save and get affordable loans. The members who save into the credit union are the same members who borrow from it and benefit from it. I do, however, feel times have changed a bit and their interest rates are not quite as competitive as they used to be. There is still a focus on their members though, which is the opposite from other sales-focused financial institutions like banks.

How does it work?

Basically, the money saved by members of the credit union in their local branch goes into a huge pot. This pot is then there to provide loans for its members. With these loans, interest is then charged. You might ask, 'Why is interest charged on your own money if you've saved?' But the interest is applied to cover overheads of the credit union, like paying their staff.

Because each credit union is run by its members, each branch is therefore independent. Credit unions have members and not customers, and usually have a great relationship with the communities they are based in.

The loans that you get through your credit union are insured, although this adds no direct cost to its members. The credit union has been known for some time to be flexible with their loan repayments for their members, although in recent years this has been rolled back a bit. There's never a sense with my credit union that there's anything wrong with savings, but the emphasis is usually on loans. As somebody who got her first loan at the age of seventeen, I held a lot of trust in the credit unions, but I worry it led me into a cycle of debt that I thought was okay.

One of the main differences between your credit union and your normal bank is that, because the credit unions are independent institutions, they tend not to have the same level of infrastructure and resources as the big banks.

My views on credit unions have changed over time. I've always been encouraged to get a loan when I've been in the credit union, rather than using the savings I've built up to get what I need. This make sense, as loans are how the credit unions make money to pay their overheads, but for this reason I do object to credit unions being introduced to children in primary schools, as I feel this begins a relationship with debt from too young an age. I feel that kind of financial education and introduction is something that should be done by the Board of Education.

Different types of bank accounts
Unfortunately, loyalty to any one bank will not serve you. I remember having a conversation with my grandad and he told me he had been with his bank for over forty years. They knew his name. They treated him well and he would probably stay with him until he died – which he did. Those days are sadly long gone. I don't have a relationship with my bank. It's uncommon that I even have face-to-face interactions with them, as it's quicker to interact online than to wait on the phone.

It doesn't mean that I don't value my bank, I just know that I value it for different reasons than my grandad did. For me I value:

- The convenience when I want to pay a bill.
- The security: can they keep my money safe?
- The cost of the fees when I want to do things, for example if I wanted to transfer money internationally. Banks can be extremely competitive.

The best way to get what you want from a bank is to know exactly what service you're looking for. But before I go any further, what even *is* a bank?

What is a bank?

We all have a fair idea of what a bank is, even if we're not sure of the full extent of their business. The Oxford English dictionary says that a bank is an institution for receiving, lending, exchanging, and safeguarding money and, in some cases, issuing notes and transacting other financial business. For most of us, our bank is the financial institution we will have the most dealings with in our lives, as they will likely handle our current account where our wages are paid, our savings account, and our mortgages if we are lucky enough to get to own a home.

How do we get the best from our bank?

Banks make their money from financial services that they sell to their customers such as insurance, credit cards, mortgages or international transfers, among many other things. There are a few things steps you should take before beginning a financial relationship with a bank:

- Do not take out a loan or any financial services with a bank without shopping around.
- Make sure that you read the terms and conditions properly.
- Only sign up to something you genuinely want, and make sure you do your research before you sign down on anything.

Glossary of banking terms

There is a lot of jargon when it comes to banking. Below are some terms that you might hear in your interaction with your bank but might not necessarily understand.

Direct debit This is a permission given to your bank by you to pay a bill or payment on a regular basis – for example, your broadband bill. What's important to remember is that the amount of money doesn't have to be the same every time, it just needs to be the amount that the bill provider asks.

Standing order This is a regular payment that you pay to the same person with the same amount on an agreed date, such as your rent to your landlord.

Debit card This is a card which you use to pay for services and goods using the money you have in your account. It also allows you to easily withdraw your money from your account using ATMs, although you will be charged a fee for this service.

Credit card This is a card issued by the bank that allows you to borrow money on credit terms. Your bank will set a preapproved limit on the card. You can do balance transfers, complete purchases, or withdraw cash. However, you will be required to make at least the minimum repayment of your balance every month. A credit card is the ultimate buy now, pay later tool because it's quick and convenient. If you use your credit cards wisely – for example, clearing your credit card loan every month (don't forget, credit on a credit card *is* a loan) – then some of the perks such as cashback offers can be very beneficial.

Store cards As somebody who is not an advocate of overconsumption, I have mixed feelings about store cards. In one sense they're good if they are for a store that you shop with regularly, for example your preferred supermarket. But it's important to remember that they work in the same way as a credit card, except that the debt is connected to that shop.

A Money Mentor note on credit cards

The biggest rule I have about credit cards is to be smart and try not borrowing money from it unless you can repay it within thirty days. Remember, when you use a credit card, you are **BORROWING MONEY**. In my experience, credit cards are best used for the cashback options that you can get with them. For example, I can pay all my bills with a credit card each month. But I would already have the money set aside in my bills account that I can easily transfer. This will give me the option of getting cashback on certain purchases. And I am using my credit card to earn money rather than as a lending tool. This would mean I am not getting a credit card because I want to use it for credit, but the perks that comes with it.

However. If you are unable to meet your payments within those thirty days and you end up having to pay the minimum payment back, you are going to be charged at a higher rate of interest. Which will make the debt repayments a lot longer to be repaid. In this way, debt on credit cards can end up costing you a lot of money in interest.

Moneylenders

This is a topic that I really want to talk about because a lot of people that I have coached or helped have, at one point or other in their lives, ended up in the trap of owing money to a moneylender. Recently, we've seen a huge rise in payday loans. I am telling you now that if you don't have to get a loan from these people then don't – the interest that they will cost you can easily amount to more than the actual original loan itself, if you are unable to make that repayment in the time agreed. To be honest, I think this is something that the central bank needs to do something about, like not giving any of them lending licences at all. There are officially licensed moneylenders, and then there are those that are unlicensed – and they are not something you want to get involved with. If you fall behind on payments with these types of black-market lenders, they will use unorthodox methods and violence to make sure you make your repayments – and their interest rates will make paying off any debt you owe them very difficult. It is not a cycle you want to get into, so avoid them if you can.

Whatever you feel tempted to do right now when it comes to borrowing money, make sure that this is something that you've really thought about. Make sure the loan is something that you know that you could repay. Are you getting the best rates possible? And before you sign anything, please, please read over any agreement carefully. Sometimes it might feel like pages and pages of boring text, but you must

understand why you're taking out a loan. Most financial institutions – like banks and money lending companies – do not draw up an agreement to benefit you, but themselves, as they are a business.

Car insurance

It seems rather strange that people feel loyalty toward a particular insurance company. If ever there was a time to be loyal to your budget, it's now. Even if you feel like a broker has given you the best deal or has saved you money by switching to a different insurance company, know that insurance is a very lucrative business. They are not giving you the best deal to suit your interest or just because they can. You have to fit specific criteria, and they have to make a profit. You need to make sure that you do not give them more money than you need to.

When shopping for any insurance, just know that you will be hit with so many different offers that it will be tough to choose what might be best for you.

It is also essential to know what can affect your **CAR INSURANCE** rates. Things like:

- How often you drive.
- The distance you drive.
- Your age.
- Whether you have ever committed a motor offence or had a driving suspension . . .

- . . . or been disqualified from driving.
- If you have any medical conditions or disabilities that might affect your driving.
- If you are a new driver.

In particular, if you are a young male driving your first car, you will see first-hand how lucrative the business is because your insurance will be costly. An insurance company will not take a risk on an unknown diver, so you will have to pay a significant premium. Or get added to the premium of a more qualified driver who will vouch for you. That's a lot of pressure financially and mentally. In addition, it's almost guaranteed that you will get a few scratches if you are still in the beginning stages of your driving journey.

When you are filling out a car insurance policy, every question that you are asked is for a reason, designed to evaluate your risk as a driver. Which is why you should consider these questions first, as risk equates to the money we have to pay.

One of the best tips that can give to you on that front is to create a sinking fund for car insurance so that you can pay for it in full. I've already touched upon why this was such a key part of my budgeting journey (no more inflated monthly instalments!), and not only is it one less bill to worry about, but it also promotes a positive experience with your car. It also gives you a sense of pride as you can pay in advance for driving privileges, and you also know you are in a position to afford it. You are now saving for the benefit of driving your car, which already sounds like a healthy way of looking at your money.

I'll be honest, when I bought my first car I didn't really shop around for insurance because I was just so happy to be driving. My insurance was well over €1000. As time went on, I bought more expensive cars – faster cars, bigger engines – and I was charged a premium for the privilege. I was just happy to be able to pay back the instalments and stay on the road that it never occurred to me that I could be ahead of the game regarding planning for mine.

My car insurance kept creeping up every year, even though I was at the max for my no-claims bonus. I had been driving for fourteen years and counting without a claim and it felt like I was not being rewarded for my excellent work. What was the point of having a no-claims bonus?

I realised that If my premium was getting more expensive, it was time for me to dig deep and look for some answers to help myself.

I considered everything – even whether or not I needed a car. I already walked whenever possible, so I wasn't just using the petrol for the sake of it, but there was no denying that in some cases, it was just more economical and prac-tical to have the car. I'm a single mother with two kids (and at the time it was two kids under two) and public transport didn't provide a significant enough difference in price. For example, considering the cost of bus fares in Dublin (which is particularly expensive), by the time I got the bus into town and back with two kids, it would only work out at maybe €3 cheaper compared with driving, including parking. But that was nothing compared with the idea of always having to lug two young children on and off the bus or walk. That was something that wouldn't be manageable for me. I was already stretched mentally, and I knew that having a car was a luxury, but it was one that I couldn't do without.

So I decided that having a car was something I would prioritise in my budget, and I feel zero guilt for that, as it made – it still makes – my life more comfortable. Many people think budgeting is restrictive; yet this is proof that a budget empowers you to be actionable on the decisions that matter to you.

In the end, what made a difference for me was shopping around: seeing what providers were out there and doing the legwork come renewal time. And since starting my budgeting journey my car insurance has dropped by over €104. It might not seem a lot, but it's still €104 in my pocket.

I also have some other tips and tricks to help you get the best rate for your car insurance:

- If you have an experienced driver in your household, putting their name on your policy will lower your premium. And they also have an option of driving your car, so win-win.
- You could always consider 'third-party, fire and theft' insurance – which only covers you if you damage another vehicle, or another motorist makes a claim against you – instead of 'fully comprehensive'. This option isn't for everyone, as it offers you zero accident protection, but it can be cost-effective for drivers looking to get on the insurance ladder.

- Obtain a quote from your current insurance provider as a new customer and see if it comes in cheaper than the renewal quote they offer you as an existing customer.
- Most insurance companies have the scope to give you a discount. Instead of just shopping around online, physically pick up a phone and call your insurer to see if they can lower the price. That tactic has worked for me every year since I started.
- If you don't get the best price with your current provider, be prepared to move on. Be firm and let them know that this is not good enough.
- There are so many comparison sites out there, so do your research!

Try to avoid increasing your excess to get a better quote. The risk is not on the insurance but on yourself.

And whatever you do, whatever you say, don't lie. Don't exaggerate. Don't pretend that somebody sharing your policy is a partner because when push comes to shove, when it's time to pay out the insurance will not give you anything if they suspect they have not been given the truth, the whole truth and nothing but the truth. Honesty is the best policy, so be honest, all the way.

CHAPTER 9:

NO-SPEND DAYS

Late one summer I was visiting my friend at her house in the country. I was looking out of her kitchen window when I spotted a giant blackberry bush a few feet away. My instincts kicked in, and shortly after, I was on a stepladder with a colander collecting as many blackberries as possible. I was transported back to my childhood in Montserrat, where there is a bountiful collection of fruit and nut trees. I'm talking mangoes, guavas, papayas, golden apples, cherries, cashew fruit and almonds to name but a few. It just so happened that the best fruits were often in someone's private garden and not freely available; but my two brothers and I made it our mission to save those fruits from rotting. Instead of looking at it like stealing, it was an adventure. Like my auntie told me, these were like the forbidden fruit in the bible.

To say my mate was bemused at my antics was an under-statement. Blackberries are a low-hanging fruit, and they are so abundant that everyone mostly ignores them. They are tasty, but they are also free, which seems to diminish their value. It had never occurred to her to harvest those berries for herself.

Many of us get so caught up in the noise that we don't realise that we have so much already available for free. We almost make life harder for ourselves than we need to.

I wonder what the blackberries are in your life?

Embracing no-spend days

How many people join the gym because they feel down about their weight? They pay their monthly subscription and are too busy to attend when they would have been better off simply walking more. How many people want to spend more time with their children but work harder in a job they don't like so they can give their kids whatever they want? Everything except their time. How many of us overlook that wardrobe full of clothes, some still with tags on, just to de-stress by shopping (even though the weird part is that the more we spend, the more stressed we get)?

What we need as a society are more **NO-SPEND DAYS** – days on which you do not spend a single cent. You don't swipe up, you don't click on Buy It Now, you don't walk into a shop to buy anything.

I didn't invent NSDs, but I have made them my own. I first heard about them online and was intrigued. I wanted to know more, so I tried my first NSD in 2019, and to my surprise, I realised that days without spending weren't just about the money; they were doing something bigger for my life in general. I began to notice a pattern: my NSDs were keeping me within my goals. I was becoming very conscious of what I wanted in my life, my financial values, and what I like to do and the NSDs gave me a mindset shift and allowed me to make split-second decisions every time I was tempted to spend. They held me accountable to my goals. I suddenly noticed just how much temptation there was for someone like me who always looked at spending money as a crutch. I became aware of my triggers and was then able to control them.

The year I cleared over €15,000 in debt, I had 230 NSDs. Coincidence? I think not. Through them I was forced to organise my finances, which was a foreign concept for me at the start, but the peace of mind it created would always make me loyal to my budget and grateful for my NSDs. They are my secret weapon to crushing overcon-sumption and mindless spending and are the key to prioritising financial well-being. Don't be fooled by the simplicity. An NSD has the power to declutter your mind like nothing else. It's almost as if you become a financial minimalist. You quickly realise you need less to appreciate more. How?

- **They keep you intentional when it comes to your spending.** They aid your focus in creating smaller habits, such as setting a number of intended NSDs for the month ahead. You set a boundary for yourself days when you won't spend, during which you won't visit places where you need to spend money, which keeps your habits in check and forces you to form new ones.

- **They give you instant gratification.** When you're paying off debt or getting into the budget mindset, everything seems daunting, and believe it or not it's nice to have little wins and spatters of instant gratification to keep the momentum going. When you reach the end of another successful NSD it is a small, but important, victory.
- **They increase our self-awareness and self-reliance.** Many of our spending habits come from the need to be gratified by external sources. When you achieve an NSD, you do so by focusing more on meeting your goals for your benefit rather than the approval of others. This also comes with the transformation of your priorities. Especially when it comes to money, you start to deprioritise living up to anyone else's standards in favour of your own needs. Nobody but you cares whether you have an NSD and you soon realise that all along you were living and spending for people that weren't taking in as much about your life as you thought.
- **They help break the cycle of living payday to payday by encouraging saving habits.** There's nothing like looking at your bank account after a no spend week and realising that you have a little left over.
- **They reduce consumerism.** An NSD does the opposite in a world that tells you to keep purchasing to fix any and every problem in your life. It allows you to pause and ask yourself what exactly is bothering you and how can you address it without

buying something? It forces you to confront the problem without the crutch of purchasing a quick fix or a product to take away your problems (especially when deep down, you know it won't).

There is so much noise right now, whether through social media, families, or friends. There is a whole marketing campaign aimed at you to encourage you to spend and we are viewed as frugal, cheap, mean, or eccentric when we say, 'Nah, I have enough.' I have been mocked and laughed at for my NSDs, but because I've had so many internal wins with them, I have become so self-assured that it became like water off a duck's back. If 'being normal' is following a trend based on someone I don't know's opinions, then I would like to be all of the above and happy with myself.

It's hard to explain the power of an NSD to someone who has never considered it, but if building a better relationship with your money is something that you want to do, then they should become a part of your routine. Building good habits is an essential part of any journey that leads to success. And it just so happens that adopting NSDs as part of your routine is my best tip for achieving better financial wellness. It's all about establishing little habits in your life that you apply to create a bigger picture.

And this can extend to mental and emotional wellness, as well as financial.

During my blackberry-picking adventure, my friend commented that what I was doing was too much work to save €2. So I explained to her that this was where she was so wrong: the blackberries are six steps away, her nearest shop is ten minutes' drive. But also, what are we paying that €2 for? Yes, we can buy blackberries from our shops, and it's handy, and they are delicious, but we are paying someone else to grow them, pick them, wash them, package them, stock them and sell them – and that's all before we get in our car and buy them. It doesn't seem like much work now when you think about it. So for me, it is also about removing links from the food processing chain.

An NSD is not about simply picking blackberries – though I do like to do this with my children once a year – it's about getting back to basics. On blackberry-picking day, the rules are clear: Mammy must put her phone down. You can't put a price on the excitement on my children's faces. We always have grand plans to make something with the blackberries, but it usually ends in us feeling slightly queasy from stuffing our faces. The best part of it is that I find my children so open in these moments, and it gives me such an insight into who they are and how they view the world.

I aim for minimum distractions on my NSDs. There is no need to worry about going off budget, shopping for food, paying bills, instead myself and my money are organised, and my head is in the game during my downtime. I do whatever activities the children want . . . as long as they are free, or have already been paid for: swimming classes, going to our local parks, watching movies.

NSDs create an opportunity for people to revisit the simpler times in their life or reconnect to something that is important to them. One client told me she has two NSDs per month, during which she bakes with her niece – a tradition that reminds her of baking with her own grandmother when she was young. Another client said she used NSDs to plan and build her business. She focused on putting money back in her pocket rather than spending it mindlessly. Another told me that his NSDs form part of his therapy as a recovering gambling addict. He has a list of things that he does on NSDs, including sea swimming. He knows that he must not touch any money on these days, and for the first time, he is starting to like himself again. This was powerful.

So what has been bothering you? Are you behind on anything? What needs to be addressed? There's no point going out and spending money when you have enough things to do at home. Make your NSD suit your own life: do arts and crafts with your daughter, give that bathroom a clean. Use your NSDs to tick off your to-do list and have quality time at home – it's a double win. Remember, when you achieve something without spending, it changes your perspective toward money and your spending habits. It helps us remember that we only really appreciate what we feel we have earned.

When our time on this earth is up, we won't wish we'd bought more shoes, or a better couch – we will wish we spent more time with our loved ones, that we'd relaxed more, connected with our children, worked less. Many grandparents lavish their grandchildren with so much love and time, and I can't help thinking it's because many didn't have the opportunity to give their children that time. An NSD gives you the option of choosing what is important to you now.

And I still haven't found better packaging for blackberries anywhere on this planet.

Implementing No-Spend Days with ease

I know that I have made NSDs sound pretty ideal – but it can be difficult to get into the groove, at least initially. There are some things you can do to help each NSD go smoothly:

1. Work out what you could be saving

Nothing offers better incentive than seeing just how much an NSD can save you, so here's my suggestion: earmark a day for your first NSD. In the coming week, track everything you spend in a notebook. At the end of the week, add up your spending and divide it by seven. That number is what you could be saving per day (on average) by simply holding back.

When I first started trying to change my money habits, I totted up my total, and although things were tight and I believed I had no money, I was shocked to see how much my total spends were coming to. Thinking of what I could save daily was often enough to get me well on my way to NSD success.

2. Make a plan for what you want to do on your NSD

Use your spend days to plan for your NSDs. For example, if I want to go to the seaside one NSD, I will make sure that I have enough food in my shop for a picnic, top up my Leap Card for the bus, sort out the tyres on my bicycle, and make sure I have the children's juice bottles and our swimming togs ready. I use my spend days to eliminate any last-minute needs to spend money.

You might say, 'Well, doesn't that mean that you just going to spend more money on the spend day?' but that is not the case; you are creating a sense of awareness. Instead of just purchasing extra, you are looking at the best way to benefit your budget. The simple fact is that you spend less money when you choose to organise.

3. Automate direct debits to go out on the same day.

Organisation is the key to NSDs, to the extent that I recommend you try to ensure your bills and direct debits come out on the same date where possible. The aim here is to simplify your budget. If your bills come out on the 16th of the month, and on that day you also do your food shopping and fill up the car with petrol, then that's setting you up for a few NSDs in which you have no temptation when entering a shop. It is challenging but very doable.

I found this particularly helpful when the children were younger. I was a single mother, and nothing was worse than having to get two children up and dressed on numerous occasions just to bring them into a shopping centre. So I chose one day to do it all. It was a small win for me because, although I felt stressed and helpless at times, I realised the power of planning. When you choose to tidy up your budget this way, it also makes it easier to spot discrepancies, unexpected charges and hidden spending (we've all heard the horror stories about the child buying and downloading apps and credits with Mammy's credit card!).

4. Create a list of things you like doing that cost no money.

The NSD is your day where you plan not to purchase anything. So instead of focusing on consumption, you can focus on ticking off your to-do list, spending time with loved ones, or just feeding your soul with whatever it craves.

I use a nice affirmation: *'A No-Spend Day is food for my soul. A No-Spend Day refuels my soul.'* Using this mantra, I can find things to do that align with my purpose on my NSDs.

Only you would know what you best enjoy doing in your free time, but to get you started here are some suggestions for your NSD:

- Call a family member
- Do those puzzles you have in the house
- Have an art and hobby day
- Do some baking
- Invite your friend round for tea or coffee
- Catch up on some reading (maybe even with a nice glass of wine)
- Finish that assignment

- Go through your taxes
- Go through your statements for the previous year
- Organise your wardrobe
- Deep clean the house
- Go and have a sea swim
- Movie nights with the kids
- Create your own *Toy Story*. I like to make mini movies with my children. You can really see their imagination jump out. If they watch YouTube at all they will probably know more about filmmaking than you would expect.
- Get out for a picnic or a forest walk
- Visit a free museum in town

5. Create boundaries around yourself.

Block all temptations, unsubscribe and unfollow any digital temptations (maybe even make these social-media-free days). Be firm with friends and family who may trigger your spending. A NSD is a self-care day and I usually spend them doing something that I benefit from. So I no longer feel bad when a friend calls me to do something and I have to decline as I've already earmarked the day as an NSD. My friends interpret it as my need to focus on my life right now and know that I'm saying *no* now so I can say *yes* later.

So stay firm with others, but also with yourself: I have learned that *no* is a complete sentence, and no matter how cute my children are, giving in to their requests on my NSDs is not worth it.

6. Don't be disheartened if it takes a while to perfect.

If you don't achieve an intended NSD, that is not a problem; it dos not mean that the day has been a failure. You might start with all the best of intentions, then realise you need to buy milk or nappies for your children. But instead of writing it off completely and thinking you have just made it a spend day, instead think of it as a **LOW-SPEND DAY**, which is still a brilliant stepping stone towards financial awareness.

So aim low at the start, once a month would do, and if you mess up, make sure to identify what happened.

Personally I now have No Spend Months. I am such an advocate of NSDs that I use them as a tool to remove distractions, such as idly scrolling websites and adding to my Amazon basket, at times when I need to focus. I use that focused time to tackle some of the big tasks in my life. When a boxer is training for a fight, they go into beast mode: their focus is on what they can do to make them better and more successful; they watch their food intake and their sleep, and make sure their routine aligns with their goal. And when I have big goals in my life – such as going from blogger to columnist, or writing my book; or going from posting on YouTube to becoming a presenter on a prime-time TV show – I too, go into beast mode. I need my brain to be in the right place. NSDs remove the temptation to spend in order to relieve these high-stress situations, and they help me balance being a mother so that I can take time for myself.

I believe that we must be careful with the words we use, so in saying, *No-Spend Day*, there isn't room to debate. This trains our brain to disassociate money with having a good time. You get a buzz from having achieved an NSD; instant gratification. Being aware of your spending habits and triggers is one of the most powerful tools in personal finance.

So why not start tomorrow? Eliminate all other distractions and refocus that energy on you. I defy you to try one and not love it. Everyone loves a winner, and the winner on all sides is you.

The No-Spend Challenge
If you find that NSDs are working for you, then you might like a bit of a challenge. A No-Spend Month (NSM) is the ultimate reset for your finances.

What is a No-Spend Month?
It is a month where you limit all spending on non-essential Items. I know it sounds impossible, but we all know impossible does not exist, right?

A great benefit of a NSM is that it can help you achieve a mindset shift around money fast and encourage you to restructure the priorities in your budget over a long period.

Some people do them differently, so it might be the case that you do not spend money at all for twenty-five days out of the month. But that is the next level up; for now, we will keep to non-essential items.

189

What do you need for an NSM?

Before you start, I want you to look closely at your expenses. What do you need to spend money on, and what can you pause for a month?

We need to know what the main priorities will be, and these are obvious:

- your rent / mortgage
- food
- utilities
- transport

Make a list of what is a priority in your life and what's a want. It is a great reference tool for when you are in the midst of this challenge.

Create a goal

Set a realistic goal you can track and achieve in your NSM. For example, I would like to create a buffer with my electricity bill, so I will aim to overpay an extra €100 or perhaps treat myself to a cheeky girls' weekend away with the money I have saved.

Your environment

Your environment is everything, so consider making this a family challenge or introduce this challenge to your friends. It's good to have a support system for motivation and accountability. Imagine how great that girls' trip would be if you all saved for it together.

Track your progress

As your NSDs accumulate, there is nothing better than ticking them off one by one. You can use a calendar for this and colour the days as your go to visualise your success.

Rome wasn't built in a day, so if this all seems a bit daunting, start with a No-Spend Day or a No-Spend Week and build up from there. Prepare for a slip-up as life happens, but just know that consistency is key, so we keep going no matter what.

I must warn you, though, that this can get addictive, so soon enough you might even try a No-Spend Year.

Mentor's Notes

- NSDs are easier said than done – you need to plan.
- Your family and friends might not understand – you need to be prepared to go solo.
- It's all right if you don't achieve a perfect NSD the first time you set out – they take time and effort to get used to.

SAVING MONEY EVERYDAY

CHAPTER 10:

FOOD

In the previous chapters, we've learned some great money habits and tips to keep our spending under control, but now it's time to think about the different ways we can save money on things we *have* to buy; how we can manage our expenses so we can put any savings towards our goals or even additional debt repayment. We want to get your money to stretch as far as possible and put it to good work.

And I'm going to be starting with one of the most crucial spends of all: food.

Food is one of the areas in your budget in which there is so much potential to save money. Before I cleared my debt, my weekly food budget was inconsistent, ranging from €50 to €150 – it was unpredictable just how much I would spend weekly. But during my debt-free journey, I managed cut my food habits in half – at one stage, when I was desperate, I had to cut it down to €25 per week. At the time, it was heartbreaking: I am a foodie, I love to cook, and I love trying different foods, and there is nothing wrong with buying the best ingredients possible to feed your family, but this comes at a cost. I had to learn the hard way that

I had to start budgeting for food in order to fix my pattern of going rogue and simply buying whatever I wanted to fill my fridge and cupboards. I had to re-learn how to feed two young children.

If I am honest, I have felt a lot of shame around this area. My relationship with food stems from my early childhood in Montserrat. My mother is a great cook. She could make the tastiest meals out of nothing . . . and she had to a few times. They were some of the most delicious meals I have ever had (hunger does that), but when I had children of my own, I vowed they would get the best of everything. Do you see a pattern here?

My aunt, who partly reared me, planted many of her own vegetables. I didn't realise that most of our vegetarian and vegan dinners were down to the fact that we didn't have enough money to buy meat. Avocado sandwiches and fresh mangoes for snacks are readily available from the nearest tree.

When things were good, however, food like meats and fish were abundant. So as an adult, having a full fridge meant that, financially, I was all right – even though I was relying on debt to buy that food, it made me feel financially secure. The reality, of course was that I was becoming *less* financially secure. So when life caught up, and I was in debt and delving into survival mode, I had to tap into and remember all of the early lessons I received as a child.

And I'm about to share every tip and trick that I've picked up along the way.

The Frugal Food Pie

The first tip is a guideline on splitting your food shop budget to get everything you need. It is an easy way of making sure you are feeding your family well, even on a low budget.

We are all familiar with the food pyramid – a guideline on the type of foods we should eat and the number of portions per day. Well, I have based **THE FRUGAL FOOD PIE** on this. I categorise my food shop in the same structure as the ordinary food pyramid only now I allocate to each food type a percentage of money that I can spend. This method has worked a treat for me and has enabled me to feed my family a healthy diet, cut back on food waste and most importantly, save money.

I allocate funds in my food shop to create great balance and variety within my food shop. It worked for me because I, like most mothers out there, struggle with guilt, constantly questioning whether I was feeding my children nutritious foods, mainly because I was on a tight budget. Categorising the foods and assigning a value on what I spent meant that I could buy my needs and wants guilt-free and improve the food choices and options that we were able to make. It also highlighted some of the food habits that I wanted to change (for example, our jelly addiction!).

So let me break it down. I have a budget of €50 to spend on my weekly food shop:

- **Vegetables, salad and fruit:** 30 per cent (€15)
- **Cereals, breads, potatoes, pasta and rice:** 15 per cent (€7.50)

- **Milk, yogurt and cheese:** 15 per cent (€7.50). This includes plant-based dairy substitutes.
- **Meat, poultry, fish, eggs, beans and nuts:** 20 per cent (€10)
- **Fats, spreads and oils:** 10 per cent (€5). You don't need to purchase oil every week, so this is an opportunity to get the best products available to you. Let that money build week after week (a good way of really getting your money to work for you is to create a fund within the food budget that enables you to buy in bulk).
- **Foods and drinks high in fat, sugar and salt:** 10 per cent (€5). No matter how high your budget is, never pay more than 10% in this area.

Don't get too caught up in perfecting the figures on the first week (it's all right to overspend some weeks) and try to only buy what you need. Just because you have a certain amount of money to spend on a category does not mean you have to spend it all. It's useful as a starting reference.

The benefit of structuring your food budget in this way is that it can save you money and force you to think outside your usual shopping basket – it is incredibly gratifying to see your family eating well and knowing you bought the food on a budget. On top of that, it encourages healthy eating habits, reduces food waste and encourages sustainable choices.

You'll have noticed that, to keep that pie balanced, you

need to buy a lot more vegetables than you do anything else (which is good for your budget too as vegetables are much cheaper to buy than meat). You should also buy vegetables in a range of colours as different coloured veg give different health benefits. Personally, I would buy enough meat for a family of three but use it to feed a family of four. I just bulk out with the veg and create a dish that is still full of flavour but is more nutritionally balanced than a meat-heavy meal. I used to be as guilty as the next person of thinking that meat means more flavour, but it doesn't. I am a massive advocate of herbs and spices, and I think the key to a tasty dish is to season well.

Obviously, it is up to you to adapt the frugal food pie to suit your family's needs and dietary requirements, but this is only the start; adjust as you go on.

Meal planning

Meal planning gets a bad rep. When we think of meal planning, we think of people on weight-loss journeys or gym buffs programmed to follow a plan. To the uninitiated, meal plans may seem restrictive, boring and repetitive.

But done well, a meal plan is not any of those things – after all, what is wrong with having a plan in motion? This is the time for us to change our attitude to things we thought we knew because this is all part of the unlearning. *So instead of thinking, 'I've got to plan my meals,' reset this to be 'I get to plan my meals.'*

A meal plan:

- **saves you time:** as a single mam I have to make many decisions daily. A meal plan takes having to pick a healthy meal off my mind. Thank you very much.
- **helps you stay conscious of the foods your family loves** . . . and the meals they don't like.
- **reduces costs:** they can be a very effective way of saving money week after week as you no longer buy for the sake of having randoms bits in the house, you buy to put the food to immediate use.
- **reduces waste:** you tend to throw less away if you've bought food for a specific meal.

To start meal planning, sit down at the beginning of the week, before you do your food shop, and ask yourself, what type of meals does my family like? What are our favourite takeaways? What are our go-to meals? Do you have any recipe books in the house that you bought but never used? Now's the time to flick through for inspiration.

Jot down some ideas for meals based on your favourites. I find eggs versatile for dinners, so at least once a week I'll have a frittata or an omelette in the meal plan, and I make sure to have plenty of veg in everything. There is no point in saving a heap load of money in planning for your future when you're not healthy enough to enjoy it, so this is something that I've consciously taken note of when planning my meal plans.

Then check what you have in your fridge, freezer and cupboards, making careful note of any upcoming expiry dates). With all of that information and inventory in mind, it's time to create seven days' worth of meals for your breakfasts, lunches and dinners. Oh, and don't forget snacks. *Create your meals around the food you already have at home.* So, if you have minced beef, tomatoes, herbs and spices, you more or less have the ingredients for a spaghetti Bolognese. So in this case, you would just need to add pasta to your shopping list.

Then just start jotting them down on a week-to-view page. It does not have to be anything fancy; a blank sheet of paper with the days written on it will do.

Meal planner

	Meal Planner November 20____						
Monday	Tuesday	Wednesday	Thursday	Friday	Saturday	Sunday	Add to shopping list
Spaghetti Bolognese	Chicken curry and rice	Vegetable soup & crusty roll	Pizza and salad	Omelette and chips	Vegetable pasta bake	Enchiladas	Dried spaghetti Chicken Crusty roll Lettuce Tomatoes Cucumbers Eggs Tortilla wraps

Getting the most from your food

Food waste and sustainable living

Saving money and being eco-friendly go hand in hand. Food waste is a global pandemic that contributes to 8–10 per cent of greenhouse gas emissions. And did you know the average Irish family throw out €700-worth of food every year, amounting to 150 kg per family . . . and that is only the food we separate into recycle bins.

How much food did you throw out this week? What could you get for €700? A holiday? A new oven, or bed, or boiler? That amount could cover your car insurance for the year.

I hear so many people give out about inflation-related price hikes on food, yet we are throwing so much of it away! So, if you are financially motivated to add more money to your bank account, you can do this simply by being intentional with your food.

Think of the production process for something simple, say a cucumber. Think of the energy put into that cucumber to get it to your table. First, a farmer had to grow it. Maybe he bought fertiliser, or maybe he found other ways of making that soil as healthy as possible so he could get more yield out of it. He then sells this cucumber to a factory. The factory wraps it up and prepares it for delivery by keeping it nice and cool in a fridge. Next, it goes to its destination country. Then it's put on to a lorry to get to the supermarkets. Then somebody in the supermarket has to stock the cucumbers on a shelf just for you to walk in and get it. And if you don't use it, that cucumber ends up in the bin. A high carbon footprint, countless hours of energy wasted in getting that cucumber to your table, just so you can just forget to eat it. It is not only costly to your pockets, but it is costly to the environment too.

There's a price for a system like this, but the more we look into the throw-away culture, the more it seems as if we throw away the planet and its resources on a whim. The machine pushes consumerism, it tells us that throwing out the cucumber and replacing it with a new one is easiest. Sure, it only costs €0.69, maybe €1 if you were to get organic, that's nothing. But if you throw out a €0.69 cucumber every single week for a year, you are costing yourself €35 annually – a minimum-wage worker has to work three hours to cover that cost. That's three hours of your time, Three hours that you could be spending with your children. Not to mention the environmental waste. Our children are watching, and they would not be forgiving of the outcome of our behaviour. Instead we can save money and reduce our carbon footprint – it's multi-tasking at its best.

Here are some of my top tips to help you prevent food waste:

- Look into the many easy methods to preserve food, especially fruit and vegetables, such as canning, freezing, pickling, dehydrating and cooking.
- Store foods properly as soon as you bring them home from the shop. If you buy meat, then put it in the fridge or the freezer or cook it. If you have certain fruits like apples, put them where they need to go, in the fridge. If you buy pre-chopped herbs, store them in a glass of water so they'll stay longer in the fridge. And did you know that onions and potatoes can't be stored together because onions give out the gas ethylene, which speeds up the potatoes' rotting process?

- Think smart. Incorporate fruit and veg into the first few days of your meal plan.
- If you're any way green-fingered, buying potted herbs is better than buying the pre-cut packet. If you are buying pre-cut herbs, treat them like flowers and put them in a jar of water.
- Keep an eye on your portion sizes. Watch what they are throwing into the bin after dinner and adjust the portion next time. Remember, every morsel of food wasted adds up.
- Buy some food frozen such as vegetables and fruits; they last much longer and can be healthy as their fresh counterparts.
- Check the use-by date on your perishable foods, and add those goods about to perish to your meal plan.
- Every food shop should be a top-up of what you already have rather than a full-blown, 'I want that because I might use it.' When?
- Start taking note of the price of foods, especially your everyday ingredients so that you know where to go to get the best deals.

Batch cooking and food prep
Have you ever noticed that pre-chopped pineapple can cost as much as €7.50, but you can buy a whole pineapple for €1? You are paying €6.50 for the convenience of someone removing the skin, chopping it up, putting it in a nicely packaged container and handing it to you so you can peel back the lid and eat as you go.

I would like to add an even more relatable example: The ham sandwich. We all love them, but how many of us can afford the best-quality tasty ham? Even for the cheapest watery slices you're going to pay more than you would pay for buying the ham fillet yourself and roasting it in the slow cooker. Which works out about €5 per kg.

That (because of the impact the extra packaging and processing has on the planet) is one small example of how I like to remove as many steps as possible when I buy my food. The products you buy closest to their original state are also usually the cheapest, so I try to avoid products that are pre-sliced, pre-cooked or covered in packaging.

In a world full of convenience, sometimes it's nice to enjoy the process of doing your own food prep. It would be so easy just to chop that pineapple up yourself, put it in a container and eat whenever you feel like it. Just like everything, planning is vital.

This is perhaps also why I like bulk cooking (also called batch cooking). Having practised the art of frugal cooking for so long now, I can feed ten people – and feed them well, feed them nutritiously and feed them healthily – with just some pasta, minced meat, courgettes, carrots, and mush-rooms. I'll just double up on my ingredients, bulking it out with a load of vegetables if I want it to stretch even further, and make a large pot of lovely Bolognese sauce, enough to create six meals for my meal plan (this is usually enough to cover me for the month ahead). I'll use some of it in a spaghetti Bolognese that night, then keep the rest aside for a lasagne or a chilli. I like to keep things repetitive but tasty – you know, make it with love once and enjoy it forever after.

Batch cooking offers a way to create delicious meals that are prepped ahead at a low cost. It's a lot healthier and appealing than most ready meals because the food is made from scratch – you create fantastic flavours to suit your taste and your family's palettes because you are in control of how the meals taste and look.

It also gives you back some time as, if you're going to cook one spaghetti Bolognese, it doesn't take much extra time to cook ten portions instead. The trick is to build it up bit by bit. I know some people who would take one day and cook every dinner for the whole month. I find that to be a lot of extra effort, when instead, you could cook like you usually do and just make sure to make more than one or two portions because you know that in the next few weeks this is something that you would have again.

Bulk-buying

Bulk-buying is where you buy large quantities of products to either get better value for money, or to be organised for the future.

Some products are more suitable than others to bulk buy. For example, I never buy just four toilet rolls, I always buy in bulk because the cost per kilogramme is a lot lower than buying in smaller volumes. But, like all things, do your research as sometimes it is easier and cheaper to buy what you need, as you need it.

Bulk-buying works best for those basic items you should have in your house at all times: flour, pasta, rice and tinned foods. But there are some items we should avoid buying in bulk, such as fresh products, unless you have a method of preserving them such as dehydrating, freezing or pickling.

So when you are bulk-buying, you need to:

- Make sure you check the date on the item you are about to buy.
- Make sure you check the price per kilo compared to buying the goods on a smaller scale.
- Check to see if the store sells a lot of this product – so you know it hasn't been sitting around for too long.
- Make sure you have sufficient storage for the item when you bring it home.

A great idea to maximise the benefits of bulk-buying is to form a group with like-minded people so you can buy in bulk together. I have clients who had told me that their parents used to bulk-buy in the 1980s when money was scarce – they would bulk-buy meat in groups to get it at a lower price.

Bulk-shopping also has a positive impact on the environment. I buy 20 kg bags of rice and flour, which means the production process is at a minimum. I get the flour at €17.80 per bag, which is €0.89 per kilogram, and currently, to buy a kilogram of plain flour is €1.19. If I were to buy twenty of these bags it would cost me €23.80, so I save €6 for each 20 kg bag I buy. Here we see that bulk-buying enables me to get a top-quality product to feed my family at a great price. It also enables me to bulk-prep (or batch-cook) meals.

But be careful, as when it is not done mindfully, bulk-buying can get you into a hoarder mindset, where you buy too much food because you want to be prepared for the worst. This is just swapping one spending habit for another. And if you buy too much food, chances are you will waste a lot of it, and we're trying to avoid that.

Pantry inventory

Every quarter, I recommend you go through your press, cupboards, fridge- and freezer and check to see what you have. I call these **PANTRY INVENTORY DAYS**.

I think it is essential to know what's going on in your kitchen, and there is no point in only doing a pantry inventory once per year. We know how that story goes: it usually ends with tins and tins of products that you thought would have lasted forever, but that you now have to dump. And the thing is, you worked for the money that bought that food, and you thought it was a good idea to buy it. So why not use it? Remove the possibility of wasting it and use it.

Also, staying on top of knowing what you have means you are less likely to forget you already have it when it comes to shopping. How many of us have brought home our groceries only to open the press and find we already have three of what we thought we needed while in the supermarket?

So, pick a day and go through your kitchen, making a note of what is already there. You can write this down on a sheet of paper or use a spreadsheet.

Grains/ pasta, etc.	Cans/ jars: fruit & veg	Cans/ jars: general	Sauces	Baking items	Beans/ pulses	Other
½ bag rice	3 x sliced apples	1 x chicken soup	4 x chopped tomatoes	½ bag self-raising flour	4 x chickpeas	2 x noodles
1 pack dried pasta	2 x peas	3 x spaghetti	2 x passata	2 x bars cooking chocolate	1 x baked beans	1 x vinegar
½ pack dried lentils	4 x sweetcorn	1 x corned beef	1 x mild curry	1 x baking powder	2 x kidney beans	1 x sea salt

This is also an excellent opportunity to look at how you're storing everything. Yes, I mean, those half bags of flour, the open packets of spices. Now is the time for you to make sure that they're correctly stored so you can get the most out of items. The longer your food lasts, the longer you have to be able to use it, meaning that you are less likely to waste it. And most importantly, this would save money.

There is an evident link between saving money and being sustainable.

At the supermarket

How often have you stepped into a supermarket to buy only one thing and left €50 poorer, carrying two bags of shopping? I can guarantee that on those occasions, you had no meal plan, did not check what did you already had at home, and did not bring a list to the supermarket with you. Or, if you did, you did not stick to it. Perhaps you were hungry.

Well, don't be too hard on yourself. It is easy to get caught up in a supermarket's relaxed atmosphere – and yes, I say relaxed. Once again, it all comes down to psychology. A supermarket's purpose is to sell, pure and simple. When you come in, they want you to part with your money. They are not afraid to use every tactic at their disposal, just like any other business.

Here are some of the most popular methods used to make you spend money and also some ways that you can fight back and be accountable for your spending habits:

The trick(s): Everyday necessities like milk and bread are scattered to the far corners of the shop. To get to them you have to pass the middle aisle, where the real temptations are lurking – the clothes section; the home-ware department; the seasonal aisle. You have to walk past so many things to get to the fruit, then you have to walk to the end of the shop to reach the bread section. And then you have to walk back to get to the milk. Why? The supermarket would like to keep you in the middle, where you pick up all those tempting bits and pieces. This is also the same reason why they keep confusing us by changing the layout just as we start figuring out where everything is, and why they encourage one-way traffic: the path they force you to walk takes you past things you haven't seen before, and the temptation is there to put them in the trolley.

Your response: Be prepared to stick to your list and buy only what is crucial. Otherwise you will spend money on things you don't need. And *avoid those middle aisles!* You did not come in to get a lawnmower, a food processor, or a new blender, no, you didn't. You came to get your food.

The trick: Supermarket trollies are huge! And they're easier to shop with compared to lugging around a basket, right? When we see a basket, we think they would be too heavy to carry around. The truth is, the bigger the trolley, the more you have the urge to fill it and the more you are likely to buy.

Your response: If you don't need a trolley, then don't get a trolley. Stick with the basket and stick to your list. If your list has only few items, then there is no need for a trolley!

The trick(s): They keep the specials at the end of the aisles to make sure that we see and are tempted by them. And they place impulse items at the checkouts. Most supermarkets have stopped placing sweets at the tills, but that doesn't mean they have kept the area empty. Instead, this is where they have the healthy foods, specials and magazines just for you to add as an afterthought.

Your response: Think about what they're offering and stick to your list. Did you come in for three cans of deodorant, even if they are three for two? Did you want that protein bar? If you had no intention of getting these things, you don't need to buy them. If it suits you, go and buy it, but really, this is intentional spending at its best. Try always to buy something based on your needs and not just because it is on offer.

The trick(s): They play on our senses by having the smell of baking bread throughout the store – even when the bakery is closed! This is the same tactic used by estate agents (the smell of baked goods makes your home appear homely). The smell of bread tends to make people hungry and tempt them into buying more – suddenly you feel like you want ham and cheese on fresh bread . . . and maybe some crisps or a fizzy drink, because it is all laid out in front of you.

Your response: Make sure you arrive with a full stomach. We tend to buy more when we're feeling a bit peckish. So the moral of the story is, eat first.

The trick(s): They give you back rewards tied to their shop (store reward points), to encourage you to go back in and spend with them. These also encourage you to spend more when you do go in as we see these rewards as free money. The purpose of the loyalty cards is to gather our data and spending habits so that they can market their products to us better.

Your response: The best way to combat this is to remind yourself to be loyal to your *budget*, not the supermarket brand. Shop where the value is, rather than getting caught up in a point system that would lead you back to a supermarket where you might be paying more. I collect points. I have tokens. I participate in savings schemes with some supermarkets, but am I loyal? No. At the end of the day, I have rewards and I claim my rewards, but only when the price is right, and that is the only reason I am in the supermarket.

The trick(s): There is a saying that 'eye level is buy level', and brands fall over themselves to have their products placed at eye level. This is also where the most expensive items tend to sit.

Your response: Simple! Check the shelves above and below eye level – that is where you will find a cheaper version of the same product.

The trick(s): Most supermarkets do not have windows. I have always noticed this, but I put it down to the supermarket needing storage. However, this is not the case – it's for the same reason casinos don't have them: windows show the passage of time. Supermarkets want to keep you shopping for as long as possible, so they remove any reminder of how long you have been inside. Similarly, most supermarkets have free parking, so you don't have to panic about how long your shop will take. You don't have to hurry because you have a ticket that is up soon. Because of this, you tend to spend more.

Your response: Try to stay mindful of how long you've been shopping. Check your watch or set a 30-minute alarm on your phone – give yourself a time limit for being there and get in and get out quick. Think of yourself like a shopping ninja.

The trick: They deliberately foster a relaxing environment. The ambience is lovely, and the music they play is soothing.

Your response: Repeat to yourself, 'This is not an outing. I'm here to get food.' Then get that food and leave.

The good news is that there are also some tricks of our own that we can keep up our sleeves.

- Try to shop without the kids if you can to avoid those few items mysteriously appearing in your basket when you are at the checkout. However, many people have offered me this advice as if it's the easiest thing to do when you're a single mam. So, if like me, you can't leave the kids at home, it's all right – instead, you have to practise saying that word, 'no'. It's a whole sentence, and your children will eventually understand.

- Getting your shopping delivered is also a great option, and there are some supermarkets who offer 'off-peak' delivery slots at lower rates (though do be wary as some require that your basket has a minimum value). The cost they will charge for delivery can sometimes be worth paying if you find yourself tempted while in store or if you live in a rural area as the money saved on your own travel costs could be a game-changer. Doing your shopping on a supermarket's website instead of going into the store gives you greater control over what you're buying as you only add what you need, you can shop at your own pace, get the best value available, you aren't tempted by the offers on the ends of each aisle, and you don't have the kids with you to throw in sneaky boxes of cereal when you're not looking!

- Check out supermarkets' own brands of labelled foods. These are often similar to the branded equivalent (a lot of them are even made in the same factories with small tweaks to the recipe or ingredients) and think of all the money you would be saving by trying something new. Yes, there may be some products that you will go back to and that's all right – you can always go back to the brand – but if you do like it, then why not stick with it? We are so hooked on brands and their marketing that we automatically reach for the brand-name version – it's the one that we know, after all – and while I've learned that sometimes value does not equal good quality, it is rare that a product has to be the top brand to be good.

- Buy based on the price per kilogramme, especially when choosing between package sizes. I've seen this done so many times where an item looks cheaper in a larger pack (or even a smaller pack if it's on sale) but when I have compared the price per kilogram (this information is usually included on the price tags on the shelves) it ends up being more expensive. For instance, I used to always buy large sweet potatoes, sold loose, but I recently noted that the smaller sweet potatoes in the packets are cheaper per kg.

- Remember that the more processed the food is, the more it will cost, and you are paying for that service. With any processed foods, you are not just paying for the food itself but also the privilege of convenience. So by getting back to basics with your food prep, you will save money. For example, chopped carrots versus whole carrots. You would save so much money by buying whole carrots and chopping them yourself.

- Consider yellow-sticker items more often – those items that didn't sell or didn't sell in time. People often ignore this section, but that's a shame as you can feed your family well from this section. If you freeze it as soon as you get home, or even prep it straight away, then you have a meal that costs you a fraction of the original price but that tastes just as delicious. There's also a certain amount of pride in reducing the amount of food that is wasted. I'm going to say it again: sustainability. My only caution here is that if you don't need it, and if you do not have the budget for it, then don't pick it up, but if you see a way of incorporating your bargain into a near future meal plan, then follow the yellow-sticker road . . .

- . . . and don't buy something just because it is cheap. Now, if it's on your list and you have the budget, then you're saving yourself money. If it's not, then you're wasting money.
- Upon leaving the supermarket, avoid picking up any brochures advertising next week's offers – they are only there to entice you back with offers you may not even need.

And the most important bit of advice of all? Do not remain loyal to any one supermarket. I've said it before, and I'll say it again, your loyalty should be to your budget! The more familiar you are with particular places, the more likely it is you will return. But you should spend your money according to value – value for your family, value for your budget, value for your goals – then you're more likely to follow through. There are so many different supermarkets around, but which one you choose on any particular shopping day should depend on what you need that day.

We have local supermarkets: in Ireland this means the likes of SuperValu or Eurospar, that are pro-quality and pro-community. Each branch is independently owned but sell products from the chain's own-brand goods. Because most supermarkets have realised the importance of keeping the supply chain as local as possible, these supermarkets are aimed at traditionalists.

There are no-frills, good-value supermarkets, like Aldi and Lidl who, instead of retaining masses of stock, have a constantly renewed selection of goods for sale and aim to sell out of these products soon after they arrive in store. Many of their products are own brand, meaning that they cut out the middleman for a lot of their food, and they work closely with (usually local) suppliers to minimise cost in the supply chain. I think of supermarkets like these as comparable to bare bones, low-cost airlines: but just because something is packaged differently does not mean its value is any less.

Then there are the vast supermarkets like Tesco, Dunnes Stores or Marks & Spencer, which are almost like superstores/shopping centres in their own right and have everything on hand from clothes to make-up to mobile phones and prescription glasses.

When money was low, the decision on where to shop came down to value for money – when your budget is so tight, nothing else matters. But now that I have a little flexibility within my budget, I can think of other factors that are equally important to me: I like to support local businesses, and I tend to prefer supermarkets that support Irish farmers and producers of products. I like to keep my money green, even if it's a little more expensive. If at all possible, I support the farmers directly.

So say it with me: 'I don't affiliate with any supermarket because I am loyal to my budget. I want the best food, the best value, at the best price, so I shop around.'

Mentor's Notes

- Planning is everything: your shopping lists, your meal plans, your batch cooking – all of it is doable with a bit of organisation.
- Use the items you already have at home to make your meals.
- Sustainability and saving money go hand in hand, so save your money and the planet by eliminating food waste and avoiding products with a high carbon footprint.

CHAPTER 11:

ENERGY-SAVING TIPS

I don't know about you, but I feel like every other month I receive a letter to say that my energy bill is going up. The cost of living is at an all-time high, and I find that energy bills are some of the worst offenders.

Luckily there are some simple things that we can do every day to bring our costs down, so in this chapter we will work through some of the highest household costs, look at how to reduce them and how to use them more efficiently to maximise savings.

Understanding your electricity bill

Residential properties in Ireland are not yet billed for water usage, but learning how to deal with current expenses like gas and electricity will mean you are better equipped to deal with water bills, and any other new expenses, that may come your way in the future. So first, I want you to understand the bills you're getting every month.

My rule of thumb is that if it is going to cost you money,

Santis O'Garro

it is essential that you understand it – I have heard so many stories of people that say they have missed direct debits because they have read their bills wrong.

Many components make up what may be seen as a simple electricity bill, so let's take a look at them.

Your account number	**950968000**	
To ask about this bill	call **1800 372 372**	
	Open Mon–Sat, 8am – 8pm	

For emergencies or electricity interuptions

ESB Networks
call **1800 372 999**
Open 24 hours, 7 days a week
Please have this MPRN number ready

MPRN 10 015 759 098

DG	MC	Profile
DG1	MCC02	2

Date of Issue	28 Sep 22
Invoice number	609736674

Billing period

5 Aug 22 to 27 Sep 22	54 days

Reading type

You meter was read

Bill Summary

Your last bill	€238.25	
Payments/Transactions	€238.25	cr
Balance brought forward	€0.00	
Charges for this period	€11.265	
Your Savings	€5.74	cr
VAT	€9.62	

Total due	**€116.53**

Pay by	**Direct Debit**	< Your direct debit is due for collection on 12/10/22. Thank You.

Term	Meaning	Explanation
Emergency Number	The number you will need to call if something goes wrong . . .	. . . for instance, if your electricity supply is interrupted.
Account Number	Your personal identification number.	You will need to give this number when contacting your supplier.
Address	The address the bill has been sent to.	It might not be the same address that the electricity is charged to – it could be a second or rented property.
MPRN (Meter Point Reference Number)	This is your specific code – it identifies your connection to the network and is unique to your home.	If you ever have a query with your supplier, or want to switch providers, this is the number you will need.
MC	Meter Configuration	Indicates what kind of meter you have.
DG	Distribution Group	Indicates what type of customer you are (e.g. urban, rural, business.)
Meter number	An identifying number allocated to each meter.	If your meter becomes damaged, this number will then be replaced.
Meter reading	This will show you what your meter is at now and what it was at your previous reading.	Different readings are used, and you have probably been asked for these: A- Actual reading E- Estimated reading C- Customer reading
Reading Type	This will indicate how your meter was read: 1. The supplier read your meter 2. They estimated your usage 3. You read your meter.	1. A technician read your meter. 2. The supplier made an estimated reading based on previous readings. 3. You gave the supplier your meter reading.

Term	Meaning	Explanation
Usage Charges	The cost for the number of electricity units used: total number of units used multiplied by the price per unit.	To confirm this is accurate, use the meter to calculate your current meter reading minus your previous meter reading.
PSO (Public Service Obligation Levy)	A levy imposed on electricity customers by the government.	It supports renewable, sustainable, and indigenous sources in generating electricity.
VAT	13.5% VAT is added.	
Calculation of the Bill	All the different charges are added to give you the final figure you must pay.	Always look at the bottom line – get to the point of how much you owe.

The best advice I can give for paying your bill is to get a dedicated bills account up and running. This will take a little work on your side initially, but I find it invaluable, and it puts me in control. Think of it as having a prepaid account set up at home. When budgeting, I estimate my payments using calculations from my previous electricity bill. Here's an example from last year:

I added the totals from all my electricity bills throughout the year and divided them by the number of paydays in the year, it worked out at €21.78 per week. So, every time I get paid this year, I put €22.50 into my 'bills' bank account (I keep a separate bank account for certain bills that offer me reductions for direct debits), so I am always ahead of my electricity bill.

Switching and saving

Now, no matter what the bill is, never renew *anything* without shopping around. I can hand on heart say that it will take about an hour (maybe even less) of your time to do something as money-saving as shopping around when it is time to renew your utility bills.

Think of it this way: if you saved €40 to €100, is that worth an hour of your time? It is not just about the money, it's the sense of control. It is another win in my back pocket, and around here, we share our successes.

There are so many comparison sites out there that will guide you through the process of comparing costs. They are so easy to use that you don't even need to know your kilowatt per hour; you just need to know how much you spent the previous year and then they will show you the tariffs available for the best value. Then you choose which tariff you want.

Before budgeting, changing amenity providers was actually a foreign concept to me. It was unheard of, a strange scenario; it was something not worth bothering with because my priorities then were not practical. However, when the money flow stopped and I had to watch every cent going in and out, securing the best deal for my family was increasingly important.

I now change my electricity provider every year and some years, I've saved as much as €150 by switching from one provider to another. Every penny adds up. And because I pay for my electricity via my bills account, I get great pleasure knowing that I can lower that amount going in every week. Even in a cost of living energy crisis, I am ahead. It's a cool thing to be able to watch the prices decrease over the years. I have also changed broadband provider, and I no longer use or watch regular TV so I have eliminated this cost from my budget until further notice. I have saved thousands at this point simply by being loyal to my budget and my dreams.

There are, however, some things to bear in mind before making that switch:

- *Before you switch, make sure you are up to date with your repayments.*
- Some providers will need you to switch to their **PREPAID** option if you are not up to date with your credit. The advantages of this are that this can keep you on budget, give you visible control over your energy usage and you won't get any nasty surprises like large bills. The disadvantages are that the unit rates are more expensive; you can't choose from as many tariffs as other bills; you risk running out of credit, which keeps you on edge as it is not guaranteed that you will always have electricity. What I really don't like is that the standing charge is simply too high compared to many other services. Is this another case of paying extra for what is presented as convenient?
- When switching, look at which payment method is cheapest (e.g. some providers will offer a discount if you pay by direct debit.)

- A lot of utility providers link gas and electric together. You have to be prepared to see what offers work for you individually. As a bundle and even with a discount, is it worth it for you?
- Find out what your **TARIFF** options are. Are you on a day tariff? Are you on a night tariff? This is important because you'll want to know the best time to use your electricity for the heavier utilities and plan your usage around the cheapest tariff times.
- Get an online bill, there's usually a discount attached.

Even if you decide to stay with your current supplier, it is worth asking them to change your tariff to the most suitable for your needs. Some suppliers have peak times during which electricity use is at a higher rate per unit. Broadly speaking, the breakdown is as follows:

Time	Tariff	Cost
00.00–08.00	Night	€
08.00–17.00	Day	€€
17.00–19.00	Peak	€€€
19.00–23.00	Day	€€
23.00–00.00	Night	€

On average, changing from a day tariff to a night tariff could save you 40 per cent to 50 per cent on your electricity costs.

Finally, if you can afford it, get a digital meter installed because you're more likely to change how you use things if you are aware of how much energy you are using (the average Irish household uses 4,200 kW/h per year). The ESB is in the process of upgrading all meters in Ireland to smart meters, which is great for your pocket and the environment and convenient for consumers. So keep a lookout for this being offered to your household. If you don't have to get a pre-paid meter then don't – simple as. THEY WILL COST MORE FOR CONVENIENCE and are usually targeting people with lower incomes.

Electricity-saving tips

There are so many tips and tricks that can help you save money on your electricity. But how many of us apply these to our lives? How many appliances/gadgets not currently in use in your house are still plugged in at this minute? How many rooms in your home are heated even though you are not in them? How many lights do you have on around the house for ambience?

Everywhere we look, we see signs that electricity will be a highly sought-after energy source: in 2019, for instance, the European Commission introduced the European Green Deal, which increased our commitment to deliver net-zero greenhouse gas emissions at the EU level by 2050. We are tasked as European citizens with a reduction target from 40–55 per cent by 2030. Sectors such as transport, agriculture, energy and the very homes we live in all have to become more environmentally sustainable if we want to meet this goal. So it is not by chance that most car manu-facturers now have at least one electric car in their fleet – cars that once would've been way too expensive for us mere mortals are currently marketed at a much more affordable rate. Having a Tesla is now more of a status symbol than a BMW or Mercedes Benz.

Meanwhile we need to be looking at more renewable sources of energy in order to achieve environmental sustain-ability, energy security, and energy equity.

The great thing is that being sustainable is cost-effective. So not only is it our responsibility to contribute toward Ireland's aim of a yearly reduction in greenhouse gas emis-sions, it is in our best financial interest to do so. And it will continue to go that way. It is now time for us to act because the younger generation will not be forgiving if we fail.

So let's get right to it. In these next sections we are going to identify where we spend the most electricity and how we can cut back.

Buying new appliances
Here are some of the top energy-users in your house today:

- oven
- washing machine
- tumble dryer
- dishwasher
- fridge freezer

- electric shower
- iron
- kettle

If you have appliances that predate the year 2000, chances are they are costing you money. Take your fridge for example: on average, a refrigerator accounts for 7 per cent of your electricity bill. So, if your average bill is €300 every two months, that's €21 that comes from your refrigerator alone.

So when it comes time to buy a new one of any of these, try to put more money aside to get the one with the best energy rating possible. Energy rating signs range from A (top-notch energy efficiency) right down to the letter G (the least efficient).

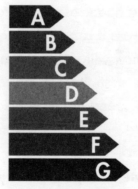

Most energy labels will show you the yearly usage in kilowatts per hour (kWh), which means the power used for one hour. It is good to be aware of this because your electricity bill is presented in this format.

Appliances with the best energy rating can be very expensive, but there are ways around that. One example is to buy ex-display – some shops sell appliances that maybe have a knock or a ding. If you're one of those people who doesn't mind if an appliance has a scrape or a little dent in it, then this is one way to get an efficient device for a lot less money. Consider this particularly for something like a washing machine. It's the workhorse of the home, so we want to put it to work the most efficient way we possibly can. Which means it needs to be more about function than aesthetics.

Either way, look for the most efficient energy rating you can afford – you will save this money in the long run. I really believe the cost per use is such an essential factor. *We want quality, we want convenience, but also, we want to reduce our carbon footprint.*

Washing machine
So, how do we save money on our washing machine?

- **Lower the temperature:** Unless your clothes are filthy, you should only wash them on a 30-degree cycle.
- **Fill the machine every wash:** Try not to ever just wash one or two pieces of clothes; always put on a complete wash. It takes the same amount of energy, for example, to wash one school jumper as it does the whole week's school uniforms.
- **Use the eco-wash function:** If your washing machine has this function, use it. It washes the clothes at a lower temperature, which in turn uses less energy.

Electric showers

There are a lot of things that we can do to save, but the shower is one of the easiest ways. Many of us associate having a shower with relaxation, so having a long shower is pure luxury (I know people that meditate during their showers) but all that hot water is coming at a cost.

I have a pump that runs on electricity and it heats my whole apartment. The last thing I want to do is reheat the water during the day. So, I make sure that I have a quick shower. For the most part, the children may have a bath and then a quick rinse off after.

So try to limit your shower time. Use a timer and limit yourself to four minutes in the shower every day. This has saved me a lot of money. One of the best tips is to put on your favourite song and when that song is over so is your shower. Now please, we are not talking a Beethoven symphony – keep it short and sweet.

Fridge and freezer

Here are some tips to help you save money with your fridge and freezer.

- **Try to keep your fridge/freezer 75 per cent full.** I have no problem because I batch cook so my freezer is always full. The fuller your fridge is, the longer your food will last (cold transfers so the items will keep each other cold). Plus, if you should ever have a power cut, this will come in handy. You don't have to fill it with food; water bottles would be sufficient.

- **Don't be afraid to adjust the temperature in your fridge.** I've noticed that sometimes if the products in the back of the fridge are almost frozen, the temperature is too low. Increasing it will not only save you money (because the fridge doesn't have to do as much work) but the food in your fridge will also be stored at the correct temperature.

- **Shut the door as soon as you can.** When your fridge door is open, you're releasing the cool air and then the fridge must do the work to recreate that ideal temperature again.

- **Organise your fridge correctly** to suit your family's needs. Get what you need, get out, and close the fridge door. For example, if my kids want apples, they know they're at the bottom of the fridge in the salad drawer. They can access that quickly, then close the refrigerator. It might not seem a lot, but we're trying to save pennies here because, as I said, these all add up.

- **Clean and defrost your fridge and freezer regularly:** we want them to work at optimum efficiency! This will also help your fridge to last longer because when you have an appliance that has to work harder to do the same job, it means you're limiting its period of use.

- **Get your vacuum out**. The wires at the back of your fridge are the refrigerator coils and you don't want any dust or any build up on them. You want these to be running smoothly. You want these to be running on total efficiency. So take a few minutes and give them a quick vacuum so they work extra efficiently.

Dishwasher

Your dishwasher is very similar to your washing machine when it comes to energy usage, but I've also done my research, and when it comes to water wastage, it is more efficient to use your dishwasher rather than washing by hand.

So here are some tips to keep its energy usage low:

- **Use it during off-peak hours:** this will mean your cost per unit will be lower.
- **Use the eco-wash option:** like the washing machine, it washes your dishes at a lower temperature, but for a longer time. By not having to heat the water so high you save energy, and so you save money.
- **Hand-wash bulkier items**: (e.g. pots and pans) as this maximises dishwasher space and helps you get a longer lifespan from your cooking equipment.
- **Scrape first:** scrape off any excess food from your plates first. Your dishes will come out cleaner the first time, meaning you don't have to rewash after a cycle again. You're being kind to your dishwasher, making it last longer.

Oven and hob
- **Match the pot to the ring size** (when cooking on your hob). If you have a small pot on a big ring, the whole ring has to heat, and this uses more energy. Such a simple hack!
- **Batch cook:** If you are going to have your hob and oven on anyway, then how many meals can you

have going in your oven simultaneously? It will cost you less in the long run.

- **Use your slow cooker:** To run one of these costs the same as running a light bulb, yet it cooks quite substantial dishes. Consider using it, for example, when the electricity is off-peak. I use mine overnight to make a stew or casserole, which prepares me for the next day. All the while, it's using less energy and less of my time.

- **Airfryer:** If you are a frequent oven-user your air fryer will become your best friend and it costs a fraction of the price to use.

- **Chop your vegetables into smaller pieces:** these then take less time to cook. I always do this with things like mashed potatoes. I just cut the raw potatoes into pieces so small that it takes me half the time, uses half the energy, and costs me half the money.

Tumble dryer

When I first moved into my home. I insisted on getting a washer-dryer combo. I didn't take note of the energy rating or the cost; all I wanted was the convenience of drying my clothes whenever I needed them, especially in winter. But recently, when I had to upgrade my washing machine, I decided I did not need the dryer. Instead, I invested in two retractable clotheslines, one for my patio and another for indoor use. Maybe you can make this system work for you too.

First, I should probably describe my washing routine. I'm on a night tariff, so it's cheaper for me to use my heavier appliances at night. The following day, I hang the washing out on the retractable line in a covered area I have outside (if you don't have a covered area, use a clotheshorse, and dry your clothes in an aerated place).

Before I go to bed in the evening, I pull the indoor retractable clothesline out. The clothes that have been drying outside all day go on this and the residual heat in the room dries out that last bit of moisture. If you have an airing cupboard, a retractable line is just perfect for in there because it takes up no floor space – just be mindful of potential damp.

This might seem like a lot of work, but it's just a routine and it saves me so much money. A tumble dryer can cost between 60 cents and €2 per load, whereas my indoor clothesline costs nothing. So I save that money every single time I do a wash. And it gets me moving.

Of course, I do understand that this routine might be harder to do if you have a big family. So if a tumble dryer is what's best for you, my top tips are:

- **Use the dryer at off-peak times:** If it will cost you less to dry at a specific time, then dry at that time.
- **Turn it off when it is done:** Most machines have a sensor to detect when the clothing is dry and will stop automatically. However, if you do not remove the clothes right away, the machine will keep going in little bursts to prevent creasing.

- **Invest in some wool dryer balls:** They absorb loads of moisture, and they could reduce your drying time by 25 per cent. Alternatively, put a small dry towel in with your wet clothes as this will do a similar job. This will save you money in the long run.

Kettle (and percolator!)

I hadn't realised that a kettle costs so much to use: at the time of writing, to boil a full kettle six times costs €0.34, and electricity prices are rising rapidly, so this cost can only increase. So to save money, I no longer fill the whole kettle just to make myself a cup of tea (something that we all do so often). To make matters worse, I also know people who will empty that extra water down the drain if they need the kettle again because they feel the water is 'stale'. They're wasting water and wasting energy, meaning that they're wasting money.

I apply this rule to making coffee in my percolator too. I'll boil my kettle with just enough for a cup of coffee, and it's much more energy-efficient than filling it to the top. I'm getting an excellent coffee cup of coffee but I'm not wasting anything. Once again, sustainability and saving money going hand in hand.

A few quick percolator bonus tips here too: I use mine as a strainer; to make tea; and to make nut milk or oat milk (I literally add water to oatmeal, blend it up and then strain it in the percolator). It's a versatile gadget!

You can also boil your kettle and pour the hot water into a Thermos or soup flask. It keeps that water for longer meaning you can have your tea on demand without a demanding price.

Heating your home

Did you know that 60 per cent of the average household energy bill is taken up by heating? There is a huge scope for saving money here, and for once, I am going to advise you to spend money in order to do so:

- Instead of jumping to put the heat on, why not jump to put another layer on? Everybody in your home should have a selection of onesies, house coats and dressing robes. You can get them brand new or second-hand.
- Make sure your house is well ventilated. Do you have excess moisture on your windows? Do they have vents?
- Look around the house and see where there are areas of damp and excess humidity. Place some moisture absorbers in strategic positions. If you can afford to get an energy-rated dehumidifier, then do. Just make sure to do your research as some can be cheap to buy but expensive to run . . .
- . . . and look at getting a professional in to make necessary repairs. Over time, dehumidifiers can be pricey to run and we are looking for long-term fixes here. Spring/summer is the best time to look at getting the work done. Like they say in *Game of Thrones*, winter is coming and it is an expensive season. So prepare in the spring/summer and reap the rewards in winter.
- Get yourself some good-quality thermal curtains. Keep an eye out in charity shops as, short-term, these could be a great solution.

- Insulate your walls with dry lining. A good carpenter can do this for you but if you are not in the position financially to do so, then start small and save towards getting the bigger jobs done.

- Lower the heat on your boiler's thermostat. I'm going to be honest with you guys, I am not very familiar with plumbing and all that jazz. But the last time I had to get my pump replaced I was told that it would be more efficient for me to do this. From that change alone (because I did nothing else), I noticed that my bills were coming in at €4 less per month. I know that doesn't sound like a lot, but that was four years ago, so with literally the turn of a knob, I have saved nearly €200.

- Heat your boiler on a timer during off-peak hours. I do this between four and five in the morning, which means I can avail of the lower unit rate.

- Get a hot-water jacket for your boiler. I have one and it helps to keep the water warmer for longer – and it's so nice to have hot water throughout the day! The water is still warm for the children's bath before bedtime, and for my shower in the evening.

- Turn down the temperature in your house – even by a couple of degrees. Get cosy, put on those extra layers (your slippers, your snuggly pyjamas) and wrap up in a blanket, because this saves you money. For the most part, all you need to do instead of turning up the heat is add an extra layer.

- Make the most of the sun! Open curtains and blinds fully in rooms where the sun is shining directly and it will help to warm your house naturally . . .
- . . . and if you want to keep the house cool, only open your windows during the coolest part of the day and close them again when the sun is at its highest (since cold air displaces warm air).

Lighting

Lightbulb moment: turn your lights off when you are not in the room.

Guys, small changes do add up. The cost of using one CFL bulb is €0.03 cents per hour, but if you have a chandelier with six bulbs in the hallway (6 × €0.03 = €0.18), and you like a bright hallway, you may leave it on for six hours in the evening (6 × €0.18 = €1.08). That's over €1 per day. And even if you only did that during the autumn and winter months (182 × €1.08 = €196.56), you are still wasting almost €200 per year, all because you insisted on having a light in a hallway you weren't in for six hours.

And if a dark hallway is just not something you are willing to accept, swap your bulbs out for energy-efficient bulbs – really you should do this all over the house wherever possible. An LED bulb costs, on average, €0.01 cent per hour to run. Your chandelier with its six bulbs, would cost €0.06 per hour. Running it for six hours would cost €0.36 a day, which, if on every night during the autumn and winter, adds up to an annual sum of €65.52.

Let's go one step further. Why not have an LED lamp or something small that will give you the light you want but at a lower price: one LED bulb at €0.01 per hour for six hours is €0.06 per day/€10.95 per year. What a price difference, yet it creates the same ambience you wanted.

With that extra money, you could be swapping or collecting LED bulbs to change over all the light bulbs in your house, saving you an absolute fortune. In some ways, it's almost like compound interest for energy: you save some money which enables you to buy the tools to save even more money.

I'll share something funny with you as well: my children will be in their rooms at random times, playing with their toys and I will just shout out, 'Okay, let's play a game. Go and turn off all the lights in the rooms we're not in!' When they ask why, I'll usually say it's for the environment. This establishes a pattern for them to be aware of: electricity = electricity users = the environment = their carbon footprint. It's also an excellent habit to get into, so we also do this when we're leaving the house.

Switching off

Before you go to bed, pull out all the plugs you can; switch off all switches.

The only thing that I could do this for but choose not to is my broadband because it's something that I use first thing in the morning. I work from home, so I want to get up and get on with things straight away.

But if you aren't working from home, if you get up and rush out the door, you might want to turn your broadband off – just turn it back on when you come home in the evenings.

There may be something you cannot switch off, and that's all right – I know that some people leave their TV boxes on in case things are set to record – but think about what you can turn off, and when, so that night times are as simple as switching the TV off, lights out and going to bed.

Mentor's Notes
- Knowledge is power – find out what the codes and abbreviations mean on all your bills.
- Go energy-efficient and buy the appliances with best highest energy rating you can.
- Make your appliances work smarter, not harder.

CHAPTER 12:

GENERAL SAVINGS

When it comes to saving money, one thing I know is that it starts with yourself. It starts with how you view the world and how you think the world views you. So I want to dedicate this chapter to you, so that you can see the various tips, tricks and ways you can save money by doing very little within your home and your life. I'm not going to tell you to stop buying clothes, or not to treat your children, all I'm going to show you is what *I've* done and how I've applied myself to spend intentionally, and, in the process, have saved myself a lot of money.

Buying a car

You will have seen from my Four Families budget method in Chapter 3 that, in some cases at least, I consider transport to be a necessity. Having a way to get to work, get your shopping and live your life is instrumental to modern living. Some people might prefer public transport as, depending on the location, they might be better off getting the odd bus, taxi or Uber when they travel. Or they might only need to use a car occasionally and so prefer to rent when they need one (though this is more expensive for an extended length of time).

But, wow, have I made some mistakes when it comes to transport . . . For example, I was the person who was always running late, so I would get taxis to work to get me there on time.

Cost to me: upwards of €2,000 a year.

I was the person who bought a car based on what other people thought: my mam, as I wanted her to be proud of me; my brother, as he had mentioned how much he loved that particular car; and my ex-boyfriend, as I wanted to impress him after we broke up.

Cost to me: €20,000.

I learned a lot about myself when I bought that car. It was an Audi A4 convertible with a cream leather interior; rims to die for. (Just let me go with this, okay?) But I didn't buy it with a long-term view of my situation, I bought it because I was trying to keep up with the Joneses. I wanted my ex-boyfriend to see me driving it, and I wanted him to think that I was doing well – but then, isn't this what's probably wrong with society right now? We think the external will solve everything. We look on social media, and we see a gold watch beside a flash car, and it immediately adds up to success. Only it means absolutely nothing.

Yes, the ex was impressed, but I was still paying over €600 per month for a car. Plus the mortgage that we'd had together. It made no sense. And there I was in a car that I hated because I couldn't afford it. Every time I got into the car I got a pain in my stomach because I wondered what would go wrong. And when something did go wrong (things were always cropping up), which is normal, it cost me hundreds and I couldn't keep up. And I didn't have the money to fix them:

- A new coil – €400
- New gears – €1,300
- New windows (someone kept stealing mine) – €500
- New tyres – €330
- Monthly insurance payment (as I couldn't afford to pay in full) – €75
- Petrol – €40 per week

. . . the list went on

And not only was I worried about how much the car cost, but I hated being seen in it. I hated the way people looked at me because I knew I wasn't deserving of their appreciative looks. People assumed that I had more money than I did, so it wasn't just my ex-boyfriend who was impressed by my car. I was impressing strangers. But the truth was, I was spending a fortune on transport because I couldn't be bothered to get up early, and because I wanted to change how others saw me.

I was shocked at my actions. And I've promised myself since that I will always **SHOP AROUND** and be smart when it comes to transport costs.

And it's funny because when you say shop around, many people don't get it. We see shopping around as getting the lowest price on something, but *to truly shop around and to do your budget justice, you need to consider not just what you want to buy, but also if you can afford it, if you need it, if you can achieve the same ends with a lower price tag.* Most importantly, are you buying for yourself or for what other people might think? I want you to think of purchasing your car the same way you would if you were to buy it for your business. Does it meet your needs, and does it fit your budget? We are aiming to get the best price for us in every category.

So when I say shop around, you need to know what you want, in the short and the long term. You need to take account of your current situation (for instance, if you're a learner driver, there's no point in going out and getting a brand-new car). You need to consider more than the initial cost of the car when it comes to affordability (and remember, you should never buy new because it depreciates, dropping at least 20 per cent of its value the minute you drive it out of the garage). You also need to consider running costs, repair costs, all of that.

For example, I later went on to buy a Honda Insight – it was time to become more practical with my car choices. Yes, I still got a loan for it, but I made sure the outgoing over the year was only going to be a fraction of the cost of my Audi. The car had to be comfortable, and it had to be safe for my children and me. So far, it has been my favourite vehicle. I got an NCT, and the car had a little problem. My stomach dropped. The tyres were running low, and I needed to replace the two in front. When I had to replace the Audi's tyres, it cost me €330. For the Honda, two brand-new tyres cost me €150, which I had already saved in my car-maintenance sinking fund. For the first time, I'd had a safety net just in case things went wrong, and I felt optimistic about the actions I'd taken to get me there.

A lot of people don't think about the potential costs of when things go wrong. Things such as:

- Could you afford to repair your car if required?
- How much is a new tyre/clutch/spare part should something break?
- Can you afford to maintain the car?
- Are you able to afford the insurance? Make sure you always check out the price of insurance for that car in advance.
- Can you afford the car tax every year?
- How fuel-efficient is it? Does it take a lot, for example? (I spent €40 per week to fill my Audi; I pay €40 per month to fill my Honda.) With petrol and diesel prices at their highest, we need to be very intentional with our decisions.
- Where are you going to park your car? Can you afford car parking? We have counties like Roscommon where it is free to park, but you need to consider paying for parking in most places in Ireland.

I know that I will never again purchase a car without considering the *actual* cost first. Like I said before, I am loyal to nothing but my budget: I want bang for my buck and I'm not afraid to shop around. No matter what my budget looks like, whether I am a millionaire or broke, I will always shop around when buying a car. It just makes sense. I understand that not everyone is able to afford a hybrid or a fully electric car, so do your research and buy the most economical car you can to suit your budget.

And it's important to commit to maintaining your car once you have bought it. I have a sinking fund for car maintenance, into which I put €10 every week. I make sure that my car is serviced every year on 29 April like clockwork. And I'm not afraid to get something fixed as soon as there is a problem.

I keep my car in excellent working condition – I always make sure to keep my tyres full of air – as, if a car has to work harder, then it will cost you more. Also, I'm not in the market for changing my car every two years. My car is not to impress anybody but myself. So for me, it is worth it. I look after my car like I wanted to look after myself.

Regarding petrol costs, not only did I make sure to choose a car that was easy on the petrol (I knew this would be an ongoing cost that was important for me to keep low) but I also make sure to shop around when it's time to top up. I do not sit in the car and leave my car running, and I don't use my car unless I have to. If I can walk, I usually do (that also means that there's no need for me to join the gym!). Fresh air is great, and I'm reducing my carbon footprint and saving money. I'm being simultaneously loyal to my budget and loyal to the planet. How great is that?

Clothes

I love fashion. I like the way you can wear clothes as an expression of yourself. I have to admit, though, I have been guilty of saying I had no clothes when the reality was, I had a wardrobe bursting with them. The fact is, I wasn't aware of what I had. Why? Possibly because, in a world where keeping up is the game's name, we can never actually consume enough.

So I say this: take every item of clothing you have and put it in a pile, Marie Kondo style, and sort through it. Do the same with your children's clothes as well. Sometimes it's hard to part with clothes because you have an emotional connection or particular reason why you bought the item.

So let's do something a little bit different with those emotions, and let's factor in a bit of practicality with that as well. Consider:

- Do the clothes still fit you?
- Have you worn them in the last year? I say the last year, because I think about the seasons – obviously we're not going to be wearing our huge, oversized winter jacket in the last six months if we're doing this exercise in October.
- What are your life circumstances now? There's no point in having a collection of four-piece suits when you no longer work as an accountant, and you are now pursuing your dream of being an actor. Look at

your clothes as either functional, practical or space-holders. Having too many clothes can hide the clothes you like.

Make a list. Take a note of the clothes that you wear and the things that you don't. What do you have enough of, and what do you need?

I have bought clothes because I've been triggered, for many different reasons. I am, after all, an emotional spender. There were times when I wanted to go out and have dinner in my favourite restaurant, but I was a single mother at home, and I had more pressing expenses. I couldn't go out, but I *could* go and buy a dress that I would wear when the time was right. It made no sense at all financially or even mentally, but it was another reason that made spending a crutch for me.

So let's remove that crutch. Promise yourself that you will not buy something on the off-chance that you might need it. So many of those clothes that I bought ended up at the back of the wardrobe with the tags still on. Sometimes you have to be in the here and now, and if you do not need it right now, why is it so necessary to acquire it? FOMO (the fear of missing out), that's why . . .

How to shop
I love fashion, but I have my own sense of style and I'm very in tune with the clothes that I wear now. I take joy in wearing an outfit once, twice, three or four times because it justifies my fashion sense and reinforces that I bought it simply because I liked it or for the way it suited my skin colour or figure.

I like to feel good in clothes, but I like to feel *good* in clothes. I'm not going to lie; I do buy outfits from high street stores, but I also buy many of my outfits from charity shops and online second-hand platforms such as Depop. I am one of those people who benefit from the throwaway culture. I made a prime-time TV show wearing mostly second-hand and charity shop-bought clothes, with a few handmade and high-street garments thrown in, and the funny thing is that no one could ever tell the difference. I love vintage clothes; also, can you actually beat the quality?

So how can you get the most from your clothing budget? Here are some tips I use that might be beneficial to you:

- **Ask yourself why you 'need' new clothes**. Before I go to an event, I tend to feel triggered to buy a new outfit. I tried to figure out what was making me feel this way and I realised that I was treating my new outfit as a cloak of armour. I struggle with social anxiety, and this spending was a way to help me cope with entering new environments. But many times that same anxiety would prompt me to make excuses to the host that enabled me to leave within an hour (I'd usually say that I had a prior engagement). It was so unjustifiable! I would have purchased a brand-new outfit for one hour.
- **Treat your wardrobe like your personal shop.** Try to keep it neat and organized, know where everything is, and take pleasure in choosing outfits that you can mix and match. We have been known to have full-blown fashion shows in our house.

- **Follow bloggers that look similar to you and have a style you admire.** This is what I do, but I make a point never to click on links that they might post. Instead, I use them as an ideas board rather than wanting to emulate their whole look. I don't keep up with trends, but I like to get ideas and looks that might suit me.

- **When you buy clothes, think of the cost per wear.** Think about how many times you will use it. Is it a garment that you will wear time and time again? For example, I have a black jumpsuit that I bought on sale, which I have styled in so many ways and worn so many times (which is unheard of in this fast-fashion world), but I get complimented on it every time I wear it.

- **Buy the best quality you can afford.** And this includes underwear. I never used to consider buying good-quality underwear, for some reason, I just thought it didn't matter. Now I make a point of saving to get the best-quality underwear I can afford. And if I can support a sustainable brand, I always will. I feel that it's almost self-love to treat the hidden parts with as much respect as the parts that everybody can see.

- **Do not buy into trends.** Sometimes trends can hurt your pocket *and* your self-esteem. For example, when I was twenty, wearing a bodycon dress would make me feel sexy. Today that same dress would not make me feel that way, so now I would only buy a dress that makes me feel sexy but also is comfortable and suits my figure. If I were to buy into a trend, then I know I would be wearing the same clothes as everybody else, which would mean that I would invariably compare myself to everybody else. I think this contributes a lot to body-shaming.

- **Buy the correct size.** You end up spending twice when you buy a size down in the hopes that you will lose weight to fit into it. I have done this numerous times, and it almost never works out. Instead, dress your body size in the best possible style within your budget rather than dress for somebody else.

I have saved so much money by applying these tips to how I spend money and buy my clothes. I know some people are more frugal, and they would never consider buying clothes that they simply do not need. For me, this is non-negotiable. I love fashion; I love colour; I love how my clothes make me feel. And although I would maybe only buy four garments per year, I make sure that they bring joy into my house by choosing outfits on my terms, and when I feel ready.

Kids' clothes

Another spending habit that I have is buying clothes for my children. To be honest, I think this is the same for many parents. We sacrifice so much for ourselves, but our children will never be subject to the same sacrifice. As one parent I know put it, 'If I can't put my children in nice clothes, then what is the point?' Can you spot a money personality here?

Santis O'Garro

When my children were babies, it was vital for me to keep up with the Joneses and to have them in the latest clothes – I once spent €40 on a two-piece for my three-month-old son, even though I knew he would only be able to wear it for around two weeks before he outgrew it. He had an entire wardrobe and I was broke – I was struggling to meet my Wall Family needs – but he had to be well dressed and well presented to the world. Keeping up with the Joneses will leave you broke. It took me a while, but I am now able to admit to myself and my kids that I will not be able to buy them the latest trends at the drop of a hat, and I don't want to either. In my view, my kids do not belong to me – I'm only a guardian who is tasked with creating well rounded, appreciative children that will fit into our society and thrive.

However, even though I don't keep up with the Joneses for my children, I do like to have them well dressed and well turned out as I think there is nothing wrong with being prideful in your appearance. I have two friends that pass girls' clothes down to us for my daughter, and I buy most of my son's clothes.

When I do shop for clothes, I go to:

- Charity shops
- Facebook Marketplace
- Sales when a season is closing out

I try to only purchase things that I *know* they need, rather than buying things I *think* they might need, either for now or in the future. With all the clothes I buy, and all the clothes

254

I get as hand-me-downs, I have a lot more clothes than I need. I only have two children, and they can only wear so many clothes within a week. It can sometimes be over-whelming, and the more I get into budgeting, the more that I realise that I want *less*. We live in a two-bedroom apartment and sometimes it can feel rather cramped, so I've become much more minimalist. My aim is now to have two weeks' worth of clothing for my children. This really works when it comes to wear and tear, and it helps me stay on top of what is needed and what is not.

On top of that, I knew that I needed to:

- Know exactly what I need to replace and when.
- Create independence for my children.
- Have a neatly put together wardrobe for them.
- Keep their clothing wardrobe to a minimum.

So I came up with something that I call **BAGGIES** – a system by which I put complete outfits into their own zip lock bags before I put them away. That way, my children can simply go to their wardrobe or drawer and pick one out.

Inside each of my son's Baggies are:

- A hoodie
- A T-shirt
- A vest
- A pair of jeans, tracksuit bottoms, or shorts
- Underwear
- Socks

For my daughter, it has been even more straightforward as she loves to wear dresses. So her Baggies are now fully tailored towards her style. She loves fashion, and now it's almost like we style her wardrobe. She's very involved with her Baggies and I've noticed that this has saved a lot of arguments when it's time to get dressed. Never mind a lot of time.

I also use the Baggies to make their activities less stressful for me – 'Oh, where is the swimming hat? . . . Where are your tracksuit bottoms?' When I'm stressed, I tend to spend money, and being disorganised means I end up buying more because I have no time to look for the things I need. When I have my Baggies, I don't have to worry about that. I'll just say, 'Grab your swimming bag . . . Grab your gymnastics bag . . . Grab a bag, we're going hiking.' It makes everything stress free.

My children love this system, and it just makes everything so uncomplicated, especially on days (or weeks!) when we are swamped. Some weeks I could be working 50 to 60 hours, and I don't want to sacrifice the time I have with them any further. And I've found that it has reduced my spending by 80 per cent. I don't just buy things because I think my kids might need them; I buy them because I genuinely know they do.

Books and magazines

I love to read books. And although reading may not sound like an expensive hobby, it can sometimes be. Self-development is something that is an excellent investment for everybody, but I've had to find ways to minimise my spending in this area. With the amount of information I consume, I can easily spend up to €40 per month on books if I'm not careful. Magazines, too, can be just as expensive at times. So I've had to practise patience and unlearn how I read books.

So what do I do? I use the local **LIBRARY**.

I've been a member of a library since I was a child in the Caribbean. I was hooked on books even then. *Huckleberry Finn* was one of my favourites, I loved Nancy Drew, *What Amy Did Next* – there were so many books to choose from, and I was enthralled by the magical worlds they took me to. I would love for my children to fall in love with these fictitious characters the way I did, but I also have to be loyal to my budget. The library is the solution.

A lot of us have library cards. But do we utilise them? Do we make the most out of the services the library offers? We all know that you can borrow books through the library, but did you know that you can also read newspapers and magazines for free? You can also borrow eBooks and audiobooks *and* you can stream video box sets. Yep, you can avail of all of this at your local library.

Now, sometimes, the waiting times for an audiobook, or just a book in general, can be exasperating, especially if they are new releases or part of a particular trend. But my advice there is just to keep a list of the ones you would like to read and put in a request for them through the library so your name is on the list when a copy becomes available. And remember, we're getting it for free, so we can't complain too much!

There are also small **COMMUNITY LIBRARIES** dotted

across the country – free hubs where you can leave in a book you might have finished, and take a book that some-body else has popped in. One of my mother's neighbours has one of these outside her house; a little box where all the books are free. It's one of the most beautiful things, and sometimes I like to look out the window and watch all the neighbours that congregate around it for a read and a chat. During the pandemic, when we all were unable to see our loved ones and neighbours, it was a way of keeping the community connected. And it was free.

Of course, there may be some books you want to read that are either not available in the library, or I'm not particu-larly eager to wait for them. I'll admit that I like to have the books I need *when* I need them. This is the case for a lot of the books I am interested in, so that's when I use my Audible account and buy the audiobook. I pay €10 per month for this service, but as I would only read/listen to about four new books per year, I can pause my account if I need to. Or I can use it to send a book to someone else if I thought it would be perfect for them to read. A friend did this for me one birthday and it was one of the nicest, most thoughtful gifts I have ever received – it was right up my street!

And of course, don't forget charity shops, guys! You can get books there for a quarter of the price. I've bought some great books that have helped me decorate my house, some cookbooks from my favourite chefs, and many others.

You don't have to buy books or educate yourself in a way that costs too much money when there are books for free or at heavily reduced prices out there.

Eating out

I love food. I love a nice cocktail, and I love that somebody has sat down and given thought to create a menu designed to please my taste buds. However, when you're on a budget, it can be tough to justify spending a lot of money on dining out, especially when you compare that cost to that of simply doing your food shop at home and cooking for yourself.

Thankfully I would never tell you not to do something that brings you joy or tell you to cut out the fun part of your budget, so here are a few tips that can help:

- **Limit the number of times that you go out to dine.** Honestly, sometimes we just get into a habit of doing things, and we lose our appreciation for them. I always think you can make an occasion out of everything, and eating out should be a happy occasion that you can afford to enjoy.
- **Choose wisely.** Many of us choose a restaurant because it's the hip place, but if you're eating a frozen burger or frozen chicken wings instead of something that a chef has put thought into, what's the point? My mother is a great cook and one thing that annoys her is when she sees shortcuts being taken with her meals because she feels that she's spending money on something that she could recreate easily at home (and probably do a better job at). So for me, I have no problem going to a

Michelin-star restaurant, or a restaurant where the chef has sourced the food sustainably and has a story behind each meal. I am willing to pay for that because I like to be educated and have my taste buds tantalised. I'm also trying to educate my children about food. I know that they like a simple burger and chips, so I at least make sure the place I choose can satisfy all of our needs.

- **Look for vouchers and see what is on offer.** If your favourite restaurant is doing a special on Groupon and you have the money in your budget, always try and get that first.
- **Go when everybody *isn't* going.** I don't mind going for a meal midweek because I think the service is better most of the time. It's less busy, so no one feels rushed, but the ambience is still usually there, and I've never noticed a difference in the food.
- **Don't pick three courses just because there are three courses**. For me, the worst thing is leaving a restaurant and feeling so full that all I want to do is go straight to bed. So, I limit myself to a starter and a main course, or a main course and a desert. In fact, if someone is willing to share a course with me, I'm usually happiest. It's cost-effective, but also, I walk away feeling that I've thoroughly enjoyed everything that I've eaten rather than feeling full.
- **Try an early bird or a lunch menu** instead of assuming that you have to go for dinner to enjoy the restaurant atmosphere.

Takeaways

I have to confess I don't use food delivery services like Just Eat, Deliveroo and Uber Eats. I'm old fashioned, and I like to ring up and order whenever I want to get a takeaway.

I was shocked to learn how high the fees are for using one of these takeaway apps – you pay so much extra per meal for the convenience they offer (up to 20 per cent more). So I suggest that you remove your card details from any apps that allow you to get food at the tap of a button.

And if you can pay in cash, do.

Also consider setting a budget that you are willing (or able) to spend on takeaways per year and stick to it by any means possible. I have a friend that never orders rice and chips when she gets her takeaway as she cannot justify paying the 90 per cent mark-up on these things, and I have now come into that way of thinking. Instead, depending on the takeaway that I'm at, I order noodles because that's something that I genuinely like to eat.

Home utensils and products

Shopping second-hand

I once paid €70 for a hob that would have cost €500. It was six months old and was being sold by somebody who had bought an electric hob for their mam, who had only ever used gas. I was trying to set up my emergency fund when my hob began to act faulty, so I decided that I would look at ways to minimize this cost. I started by looking at adverts on Facebook Marketplace and was shocked to see what was available. Yes, it was risky because I couldn't return it, but shopping second-hand is always a risk worth considering. It's now three years later, and I have never had a problem with that hob.

I also bought a sideboard second hand. It cost €80 and it was beautiful. It was fifty years old and more than I could have wanted. I had seen something similar in IKEA for €700, but sometimes the things we buy and think of as new or in fashion are replicates of things already out there at a lower price. Things that other people are trying to get rid of because we're all caught up in this pattern of consumption in which everything must be new.

If you look at the world differently, you look at products, utilities and tools differently, and you can capitalise on this. I couldn't believe what was out there.

I had spent seven months looking for three stools to fit under my breakfast counter. I eventually found them in Adverts.ie (a preowned selling site similar to Facebook Marketplace) for €70 and everybody that enters my house for the first time compliments me on these stools. If I'm honest, I'm a little bit smug when it comes to these stools as not only can no one else get ones like mine now, but those that are available are made at a quarter of the quality, but sell for double the price that I paid for three.

And you don't have to stop at the big items, either. None of my plates match each other because I purchased them from charity shops, or from places like TK Maxx.

I like pretty plates, but buying a whole set can be so expensive, and then I feel like I'm stuck with just one theme. So instead, I mix and match my plates and my cups. And then I'm not limited to where I can acquire them. I have mugs in every colour, and I've noticed that when friends and family come over, they all seem to pick a mug that ties in with their personalities.

I know that this tip may not be for everyone – my friend once told me they thought it was unhygienic to purchase plates from charity shops, but my response was to ask whether they thought restaurants buy new cutlery and plates every time they have new customer? No, they wash, dry, and reuse them, which is the same thing I do when I purchase from a charity shop.

If I had been keeping up with the Joneses, I probably would have thought I was doing something wrong, but I don't. And I save a lot of money as I host a lot of dinner parties and gatherings with my family and friends. And I entertain in a way that pleases me. When I see somebody using a plate that I've chosen specifically to put in front of them, it brings me such pleasure.

I'm not saying everybody needs to do this particular tip, but I am saying that there are ways to think outside of the box, literally and figuratively.

My final bit of advice regarding homeware is to use (and reuse) what you have. You may feel you have to go out and buy a fruit bowl just because it's *called* a fruit bowl, but why not use that large pasta dish that only comes out once every year or two when you decide to have an Italian night?

Why not show off all your pieces and make every day a special occasion? A fruit bowl is what you make it, and when you understand the concept of marketing and listen to what you're being told, you will realize that you can rewrite the narrative around most things *and* save yourself money.

Hygiene and personal care

Women's hygiene products are a lifelong expense for half the population, yet they don't get half enough attention or recognition as a cost in our lives. Tampons, sanitary pads and wipes can add up to quite an amount over a lifetime. So I found a cost-effective way of challenging this. Going down the sustainable route has already saved me hundreds, and If I am honest, it feels a lot more hygienic and comfortable. While I feel that I am late to the game in making these changes, I feel like I must pass on what I've learned to you, my reader.

We often view new products, fresh out of the wrapper, as cleaner and healthier for our bodies, but sometimes that isn't the case: many of us have heard of how tampons can increase the risk of toxic shock syndrome by being either super absorbent or left in too long. Or the fact that when you're removing your tampon, the fibres can stick to your vaginal wall, causing abrasion.

What I've found is that what matters to me is not having a new product; it's also about using a sustainable product that looks after your body (and also the environment!). Remember, if you look after your health, you also save money in the long run. Your health is your wealth, as they say. So here are a few products I've been using that have saved me quite a bit of money in a short amount of time.

The first thing I did was swap my usual tampon for a menstrual cup. Menstrual cups are widely available, and they can start from €11 and go up. They are reusable, and the funnel shape is rubber or silicone. Although they are flexible for insertion, and you use the tab at the end for removal. They can be worn for up to twelve hours. For younger women, you should use a smaller or a beginner cup. If you're over thirty or have given birth, use the heavier cup.

The best thing about these cups however, is that they can last up to ten years. So multiply how much you spend on tampons every single year by ten. And think of the price you would spend purchasing one or two cups that would last you ten years. Not to mention how much waste you are saving by not buying and discarding tampons, pads and their packaging.

My other go-to are period pants – they are so comfy! If you're like me and have had children, sports such as skipping and yoga can cause a little bit of leakage. Period pants give me peace of mind when I'm doing these activities, and also when I'm going to bed during my menstrual cycle as there's no chance of a leak. Although, of course, I've never leaked with a menstrual cup, I like to be reassured and wearing the period pants feels comfy. They're an alternative to having in a maxi pad, and you can keep them up to twenty-eight washes.

In terms of other products, I do tend to look out for reusable alternatives to disposable items that I use regularly. For example, instead of wipes, I always use a washcloth. There are also so many different types of make-up removers, gloves and mitts that you can place in your washing machine and are ready to use again. It's the same for non-plastic cotton buds and razors you can change. I don't mind spending the money upfront if I know it would save me in the long run. They might seem expensive to purchase at first, but in the long run? You're saving yourself a lot of money when you add it all up (and again, making things easier on the environment as you're reducing waste).

The garden

I love gardening and most of the tips that I'm about to give you, I got from my mother, Rosie. Everybody comments on my mam's garden – it's a work of art, and sometimes I think it could almost be her first child. I promise no jealousy here! But my mam gardens because it is her escape, and she finds it good for her wellbeing.

This is how Rosie saves money on her garden:

- She collects seeds from previous plants to use them the next day.
- She swaps seeds with other people.

- She is never afraid to split plants and multiply them that way.
- She will often ask her neighbours (and even random people) if she can take a sprig from a plant in their garden so she can plant it in hers.
- She uses recycling for her plant pots: empty milk cartons, egg trays, tins . . . you name it, she has used it.
- She uses the water she collects from the garden shed and the back of the house for her plants.
- She prefers that people give her fruit trees and potted plants for the house instead of flowers. When Mother's Day comes, or her birthday, or if we want to give her a thank-you gift we know better than to buy my mother flowers. Instead, the plants she receives stay with her for years and years as she is so green-fingered. And we end up enjoying their beauty or eating their fruit for years to come. All with a story attached.

I asked my mam what her top tip was, and she said, 'Don't be afraid to ask.' She told me that Dublin City Council, for the most part, only use most of their bulbs for one year only because of fear that they won't bloom the following year. My mam has no shame in asking for their discards, and each spring, she gets a surprise crop of daffodils and tulips, using varieties that she couldn't possibly afford to buy in the shop.

And now, thanks to her, I can use varieties that I would have never thought of.

My mam is not a master budgeter, and she wouldn't be as money-conscious around many things – I guess now she doesn't have to be – but when it comes to her garden, she has shown me another way in which being frugal does not mean that you're being limited.

Now here is a challenge for you – what can *you* do to reduce in all of these areas? What ideas would you have when it comes to making savings at home? What are some of the things you purchase without even considering whether they can offer savings?

CONCLUSION

It is only fitting for me to conclude this book by saying the same thing I did at the start – to be good with money, you have to start with your mindset. It's how you view the world and how you view yourself that truly impacts how you view your money. I got into a negative cycle of debt because of a few key influences:

- How I viewed myself.
- How I viewed my environment.
- The expectations of society.
- My greediness.
- The feeling that I needed to keep up with the Joneses.
- My lack of financial education and awareness.

I stayed in the negative environment and the negative patterns of financial behaviour for longer than I needed to because I didn't have the know-how, the education or the mindset to start the process of change.

I don't have a magic wand. I don't have a superpower. What I do have is an awareness that one size does not fit all and that it wasn't one single thing that I did that changed my relationship with money. It was a whole set of changes

– changes of habit, of mindset, of behaviour – that I hope to have brought together in this book. It wasn't easy for me to make the changes I needed to make; it was uncomfortable and emotional at times. But it was possible. What's important to remember is that, to understand how to get out of a situation, you have to face the question **'HOW DID I GET HERE?'**

We endure hardships and face challenging financial times. It's important for you to remember though that you can make it through any financial difficulties with the right help. And with the right mindset, you can ultimately make the proper steps to lead you toward your goal.

I still have a long way to go in my learning process, but one thing I know is **IF I CAN MIND MY MONEY, I CAN MIND MYSELF**. If I'm going to be loyal to anything in this world I'll be loyal to my budget, because being in debt can be the biggest block to your financial freedom.

What I would recommend, if you found this book useful, is to continue reading books like this one. There are no stupid questions that you can ask. If you don't know, the stupidest thing that you can do is *not* ask and find out.

ACKNOWLEDGEMENTS

I want to firstly thank you, the reader, for reading this book. I want to thank the team at HarperCollins Ireland. Many thanks to my friends and my family who supported and encouraged me to keep writing even when imposter syndrome had set in, and I didn't feel capable of putting another word on that screen.

Is it a huge deal for a young black Caribbean woman to have this opportunity, and I'm so proud to be able to spread what I've learned and hopefully help others in some small way, making financial literacy available to all.

FURTHER READING

- Commission for Regulation of Utilities, *Annual Report, 2017* (CRU, 2017) www.cru.ie/wp-content/uploads/2019/02/Commission-for-Regulation-of-Utilities-Annual-Report-2017-Final.pdf
- Healthy Ireland, *The Food Pyramid* (Department of Health, 2019), www.gov.ie/en/publication/70a2e4-the-food-pyramid/
- Honda, Ken, *Happy Money: The Japanese Art of Making Peace with Your Money* (Simon and Schuster, 2019)
- Kondo, Marie, *The Life-Changing Magic of Tidying* (Vermilion, 2015)
- Organisation for Economic Co-operation and Development, *How's Life? 2020: Measuring Well-being* (OECD, 2020)
- Ramsey, Dave, '7 Baby Steps', www.ramseysolutions.com/dave-ramsey-7-baby-steps
- Warren, Elizabeth and Warren Tyagi, Amelia, *All Your Worth: The Ultimate Lifetime Money Plan* (Simon and Schuster, 2005)
- Ware, Bronnie, *The Top Five Regrets of the Dying: A Life Transformed by the Dearly Departing* (Hay House, 2012)